Grace at This Time

Grace at This Time

Praying the Daily Office

C. W. McPherson

MOREHOUSE PUBLISHING

Copyright © 1999 by C. W. McPherson

Morehouse Publishing
P.O. Box 1321
Harrisburg, PA 17105

Morehouse Publishing is a division of The Morehouse Group.

Printed in the United States of America

Cover design by Trude Brummer

Library of Congress Cataloging-in-Publication Data
McPherson, C. W.
    Grace at this time:praying the daily office / C. W. McPherson.
        p.   cm.
    Includes bibliographical references.
    ISBN 0-8192-1784-0 (pbk. : alk. paper)
    1. Episcopal Church. Book of common prayer (1979). Daily office.
2. Divine office. I. Title.
BX5944.D23M36   1999
264'.03015—dc21   99-34670
                                                                        CIP

Contents

One Friday Morning
in Early October

I was glad when they said to me, "Let us go to the house of the Lord!"
—Psalm 122:1

Four of us gathered in the chancel this morning. Martin is a young musician and technician for musical instruments. Michael is a local policeman. Martha is a retired teacher from a Caribbean nation who has worked for many years in the United States. I am the rector of a small parish church. We each had only a few minutes, so we came dressed for work. In appearance and affect, we could scarcely have been more different: Martin in his dusty work clothes, Mike in his crisp and clean blue uniform, Martha in sweatshirt and jeans, me in my jacket and clerical collar.

But in that few minutes, we experienced a great deal. We prayed a prayer of Augustine (fourth century), a prayer from Reformation England (sixteenth century), a prayer from the earliest church (first or second century), and said a litany made up of verses from the Psalms (going back to 1000 B.C.E.). We chanted three entire Psalms, plus two other biblical songs, and we read two Bible lessons. We renewed our faith, employing the words of the oldest intact Christian creed. We shared aloud, with God and one another, our concerns about matters near and far, our fears and frustrations. And we also thanked God for many blessings—not the least of which was the gift of one another. We also spent several minutes in silent meditative prayer. In all, it was a wonderful way to start a busy Friday at the end of a hard week's work.

So where were we? On retreat? At some cathedral? At an interfaith center? What was the occasion? An ecumenical event? A diocesan or other convention? A visit to a monastery or convent? Were we getting ready for a workshop at a seminary, or getting a head start on a renewal weekend? And who were we? Committee members? An interreligious task force? A diverse vestry? A search committee? Members of a Third Order?

None of the above. We are not members of the same parish—not even the same diocese—and we serve on no committees in common. We share no common identity, other than Christian—we are not even all Episcopalians. We went our various ways the rest of the day. Two of us have been delegates to diocesan conventions, the other two have not. As it happens, none of us has ever been an elected vestry member. Only one of us is a cradle Episcopalian; among us we have practiced atheism, Buddhism, and Judaism. Three of us at present are practicing Episcopalians, although only two have been confirmed. One more thing should be added: I was the only ordained person in the group, but I was not the leader. It was Nancy's turn.

What were we doing?

All we were doing, all we did, was to pray Morning Prayer together in the chancel of our local parish church, using no resources beyond a Bible and four prayer books.[1] And although it was a wonderful way to start the day, it was not unusual at all. It was in no way a special version of the service: there were no unusual embellishments, and it was not a special feast day or anything like that. It was just morning. We—that is, variations of this group—start every day this way, Sunday through Saturday. We are not always together—three days in the week, for example, I pray the Office somewhere else—but we use the same form and the same two resources. Why do we do this? All the reasons gather into one—because we love to do it.

Why? To begin with, the service is in its remarkably varied constituent parts a rich and rewarding experience. On any given day, the same elements would be present, but the content would be different. We might use prayers by different masters of the spiritual life, from different ages, and from all round the world; lessons and songs from throughout the Bible; and individual concerns ranging the alpha and omega of human experience.

On another level, the service offers us a moment of silence and sanity. On any given day, the silences, the Creed, and the Lord's Prayer will be present, lending calm and continuity and centering to our chaotic contemporary lives. We find a quiet strength in that, and quiet strength is a rare commodity.

Yet again is the corporate aspect. The group I describe is typically diverse for our parish, but that only begins to suggest the human diversity the Daily Office can address. Once people get to know the Office, they realize that its practice puts them in touch with a vast community of like-minded—and not so like-minded—believers throughout the world, and through the ages. I tried above to suggest some of this richness, but more remains to be said. Morning Prayer, practiced regularly or daily, is one of the most powerful symbols and experiences of ecumenical unity that Christianity has ever evolved.

In a word, we are all involved in, attracted by, and committed to the discipline of the Daily Office. But not in the modern senses of the word *discipline* as something necessarily "strict," or as an equivalent word for "punishment." On the contrary, the Office is almost never *strict* in any sense of that word I know, and rarely painful. We are involved in the discipline because it is, for us, an excellent expression of our discipleship. The Daily Office teaches, forms, and equips us for ministry, and for daily life. One of the least pious and most casual seminarians I ever met once admitted to me that, although he disdained requirements, he often went to Morning Prayer because "it makes your day go better." Those of us who pray the Office could not agree more, and that is one reason we have developed this discipline.

Moreover, the practice day by day perfectly expresses our religious identity. It not only reminds us of exactly who we are, and exactly what we need to do, but also strengthens us to do it. As Augustine said, the Daily Office helps us "become what we are"—baptized men and women. It expresses our theology, deepens our spirituality, gives us a daily experience of our biblical taproots, encourages our intercessory prayer life, and connects us to one another—to persons praying the Office around the world—and to our eucharistic and sacramental life.

At this point a reader might ask, "Are you really aware of all these elements every time you pray the Daily Office?" The answer is no; not all of it, not always. But more often than not, a great deal of this awareness dawns on the regular practitioner. Morning Prayer, Evening Prayer, and their variations take on a life of their own; the Office becomes a habit and, more than that, a vital part of daily living. Those of us who enjoy it daily really do love it. To continue in a daily practice we must love it, at least at some level.

From the opening verse, "Lord, open our lips," to the concluding blessing, "Let us bless the Lord," the Office has that mixture of deep feeling, beauty, relevance, and comfortable familiarity—balanced by delightful variety, understanding, and expectation—that is often involved in love. Comparing notes with others who have practiced the Office for years has confirmed this idea. Those who practice the Office long enough to become proficient, long enough to know how to pray it and not simply to say it, always come to love it.

Yet this is not what the Office represents to most people. As far as the Daily Office is concerned, the current edition of the *American Book of Common Prayer* is underemployed. Most faithful churchpeople seem to know and use only limited portions; the greater part remains unopened and unknown.

The Daily Office, although it is the first item in the book, seems familiar to the majority of worshipers in only two ways: as a principal Sunday service, on the one hand, or as a special practice for clergy and monastics. Neither of these uses represents the original intent for the Office, although, obviously, it can be used in these ways. It is as if one used a new automobile exclusively as a water heater, or a new computer as a depository for grocery lists: they can be used in those ways, but these would seem bizarre restrictions. We would say that such a car, or such a computer, is "underemployed." Very few Episcopalians seem to think of the Daily Office as intended for *all baptized persons*, to be practiced on *a daily basis*. Yet from its very name that is its nature and purpose.

A number of historical and other factors have contributed to this neglect and misunderstanding, many of which we will examine shortly. But it may be that many people think the Daily Office is complex, difficult, and time-consuming. It is not, or at least it does not have to be. It is designed to be easy to manage and brief. It should take a few minutes' time at the most, and requires no special training, much less formal theological education, to manage. I practiced the Office long before I had formal theological training.

And while I must deal occasionally with complex, time-consuming, and difficult tasks, as most people must, I certainly would not choose such tasks as part of my daily life.

The conviction that leads to this writing, then, is very simple: a vast majority of people are missing a valuable gift in the Daily Office. I am thoroughly convinced that, if more people knew about it, tried it, and grew to understand it, the Daily Office could be a blessing for laypersons, bishops, deacons, and priests throughout the Christian church. But in my experience at least, few people seem to know about it, fewer still have tried it, and fewer still understand it.

This work is intended first for that vast majority who know very little about the Daily Office, Morning Prayer, Evening Prayer, and their useful variants, the Noonday Office, Compline, and the Devotions for Individuals and Families. I will try to provide the necessary background information truly to *introduce* the Office: its character and virtues, its history, its theology, its spirituality, its component parts. I will try also to provide practical suggestions for implementing the Office in the parish, and above all in individual life. I believe that the *Book of Common Prayer* is "user friendly," much more so than any computer I have ever seen. But the fact is that many people find the book daunting, hard to figure out. Therefore, I will try to provide instructions and suggestions written with the intelligent but uninformed churchperson in mind.

The book is intended equally for those already in the process of discovering the Daily Office—individuals and small groups and parishes who have intuited the value of this classic Anglican approach to spirituality, and who have begun praying the Office on a regular basis. There are many such people in each of the four principal ministries of the church. I hope this book will encourage them to further their journey, and help deepen their experience of the blessing they have already found. For both categories of readers, a long section entitled " 'Who Gets to Do This?' A Colloquium on the Daily Office" is included as an appendix. This section addresses problems a variety of laypersons and persons in various Orders have encountered in trying to practice the Office, or in planning to practice it.

Finally, the work is intended as a course of new knowledge and challenge for those who already have made the Office a long-term part of their spiritual life. The anthropological reflections in the initial chapters, the theological chapter, and the chapter on spirituality are almost entirely original. Even in the historical materials such persons may find helpful information. In introducing and teaching the Office I have often heard the comment, "I've used Morning Prayer for years, but I never knew exactly where it came from."

I trust, above all, that anyone who has prayed the Office simply, faithfully, and on a daily basis for any substantial length of time will agree with the deeper thesis of this book: the Daily Office, once faithfully practiced, involves all the benefits and blessings of a long-term relationship or commitment, such as learning mastery of an art or craft, participating in an exclusive relationship, or raising or educating a young person.

In other words, the Daily Office calls for a sense of humor, centered strength, and patience. It is priceless.

The Daily Office and Daily Living

From the rising of the sun to its setting my name is great among the nations.
—Malachi 1:11

In the previous chapter, I introduced with some trepidation the idea of the Office as a daily practice. I know what that may have suggested to many readers: daily "church." The inference is that the Office involves a heroic commitment of time and effort, appropriate for "specialists" of some sort (monks and priests again), but not relevant for those who have busy lives in a "real world." The idea may also suggest to the many unfortunate Christians taught from an early age that worship is primarily a matter of "duty," that the Daily Office is good for you, like bitter medicine or drudgery. If that is what the Daily Office were like, I would not wish it on anyone, and I would not do it myself.

These are understandable first reactions to the idea of praying the Office regularly. I hope, however, to share a practice that I and others have found eminently practicable and almost always enjoyable. Before I offer some concrete (and, I hope, modest) proposals, let me try to provide a framework for understanding the Daily Office.

There are certain tasks—getting dressed in the morning, cleaning, and grooming—that we do every day. Indeed, because we perform these tasks so often, we take them for granted; most of us give them little thought. Insofar as they need to be taught at all, most people learn these things at a very early age and find them therefore almost thoughtlessly easy to do. Most of us would even be tempted to call such tasks "natural," or instinctive. But they are not. Once upon a time, we had to learn them.

Other things, by contrast, we do as part of a weekly routine. These tasks might include employment, formal entertainment, dining out, sports events, religious services, and trips to the library or the grocery store. For most people these are more obviously culturally conditioned or learned behaviors, and nobody would be tempted to think of them as "natural." Yet they, too, are so often repeated that we take them for granted and can accomplish them without a great deal of planning and deliberate effort.

Then there are activities that recur only on a yearly or seasonal basis: religious and family celebrations, reunions, seasonal chores such as raking leaves, shoveling snow, tending gardens, mowing grass. Familiar though these tasks are, they must always be partially relearned. This gives them a quality of newness each time they are encountered. They are in this sense like the events that occur only occasionally, such as weddings and deaths, births and disasters. The latter can never be learned, only remotely anticipated. They can be foreseen, but not predicted, and therefore for most humans have an aspect of the uncanny. They interrupt our lives, rather than supporting life's rhythm. By definition, such events cannot become routine.

All of these are among the ways we experience *time*. The ancient Greeks saw that the experience of time varies greatly according to what we are experiencing. They therefore distinguished between *chronos* or clock time (whence our English word *chronological*) and *kairos* or seasonal time. Our daily lives, and the events mentioned in paragraph above such as washing and dressing, are matters of *chronos*; they are what T. S. Eliot's Alfred Prufrock means when he cynically mentions "measuring our life in coffee spoons." Occasional events, whether sporadic and unpredictable, like pregnancies and illnesses, or regularly recurring, like Christmas and birthdays, are *kairos*. This is a basic Judeo-Christian distinction as well, expressed in mythical language in the Old Testament. According to Genesis 1:14, the stars in the sky are there to define the seasons, that is, to establish *kairos*. The alternation of light and darkness on a daily basis follows next, establishing *chronos*: such periods define the ordinary day and night. Chronological experience is more or less rigidly timebound. We tend to eat, sleep, and work—all daily activities—"on time." *Kairos* events are comparatively time-less. We do not "notice" time when we are intensely absorbed, when we are "having a good time" (as at a birthday party), or when events are ritually and impressively solemn (as at a funeral). Finally, chronological events tend to be repetitive, "the same." However varied our wardrobe, we tend to wear the same sorts of clothes every day. We tend to drink and eat the same foods, and so on. *Kairos* events tend toward differentiation and novelty, so that, however much certain elements are repeated, every birth and every death is manifestly distinct—as, to a lesser extent, every birthday and every Good Friday is different.

The church mirrors this structure of time, which makes sense for an incarnational faith. We have seasons—Lent, Epiphany, Advent—that are distinctive, annual, and experienced as novel, to an extent, each year. We have ritual and theological approaches to the occasional and random event, the crises of birth, marriage, illness, death. Even nonchurched people are aware of these events, even those who know only about the commercial Easter and Christmas. The church marks *kairos* time very well.

What about worship in chronological time? Put another way, what constitutes the experience of religion for most people? In the majority of mainline, traditional denominations, weekly worship in recent centuries has become the norm—we worship on Sunday, the Lord's Day. As a result, in the minds and consciousness of most, attendance at church has become the primary religious requirement, the extent of most people's theological *chronos*.

Most denominational Christians practice daily worship, if at all, in an extremely attenuated and perfunctory way. They may "say their prayers" at bedtime or in the morning, or "say grace" or "the blessing" at mealtimes. These prayers may incorporate a more-or-less brief intercessory list, perhaps the Lord's Prayer or Our Father, perhaps a confession of sin. Often people have a sense that praying "in your own words" is better than set forms. Perhaps the prevailing informality of contemporary culture, its anti-intellectual and antitheological bias, all support such habits as well.

At the same time, many adults have experienced a lack in their individual prayer lives and in daily religious experience. They have therefore found themselves drawn to other traditions in an effort to find a *chronos* sense. Or to put it more simply, many have felt the need for intentional, daily spiritual practice. Some years ago a trend began, which continues to this day, of experimenting with the Hindu tradition of the mantra-prayer and transcendental meditation. Various Buddhist disciplines and practices, especially centered around Zen, have attracted Westerners in general and Christians in particular for some time now (at least since the Beat movement of the 1950s). At the same time, the charismatic and evangelical traditions, with their emphasis on individual piety and enthusiasm, seem to encourage daily spiritual experience, and, paradoxically, to demand a daily formal observance mysteriously absent from the practice of more traditional denominations.[1]

I say "paradoxically" and "mysteriously" deliberately, since the Anglican tradition, and to a lesser extent the larger Catholic Christian experience of which Anglicanism is a part, has always offered a particularly rich, convenient, even ingenious approach to daily devotion. The approach has an ancient Christian pedigree and has been basic to the spiritual formation and identity of our most conspicuously self-sacrificing saints, leaders, and teachers. We have always known how to mark chronological time, by offering a tradition that sanctifies the ordinary day for the ordinary Christian with a comprehensiveness and thoughtfulness perhaps unknown in any other Christian tradition.

That tradition is that of the Daily Office. It was originally intended to be the most often used and the most widely practiced element in the *Book of Common Prayer.* That is the reason the Office appears at the beginning of the book, after the preliminary calendars and so on. The Daily Office is intended for the whole church—every single member—every single day, which is why it is short in its essential form. This is a matter of fact, not opinion: the intention was to offer a daily form for devotion that everyone could use. Yet the Daily Office is at best marginally understood, and practiced, by the great majority of Anglicans.

When I sketch the history of the Office in chapter 1, I will explore why the Office has become so widely misunderstood, misapplied, and underused, and why, loosely and sporadically, it is beginning to show signs of rebirth. At this point, an easy way to understand the practical nature of the Office is to examine the contents of the *Book of Common Prayer* (pp. 5–7).

Four types of material appear: (1) Collects, prayers, thanksgivings, and psalms, which are to be incorporated into various services; (2) miscellaneous tools for instruction and edification—the catechism and the historical documents; (3) the calendar and the lectionary, which are tools for designing proper and timely services; and (4) the services themselves: Morning and Evening Prayer, Eucharist, proper liturgies for special days, baptism, pastoral Offices, and episcopal services.

The latter correspond to the various mundane activities I began to discuss earlier in this chapter. Baptism happens only occasionally. It happens "to" individuals only once in a lifetime, and it happens within the parish family on an unpredictable basis. Weddings, funerals, and the other services under the "pastoral" heading similarly happen on an occasional basis; the same holds for episcopal services, which in many places do develop a "yearly" quality in that they correspond to the bishop's visitations to parishes and his or her schedule of cathedral events. The liturgies for special days are all once-yearly events, like secular birthdays and anniversaries. The Eucharist has for two millennia been the main weekly celebration for the Lord's Day, and secondarily the basis for most of the other services we have enumerated so far.

The Daily Office—first and foremost—is the daily observance of the church, comparable to daily activities like tooth brushing. To state the obvious, that is why it is called "daily." Once understood, the Office is in several ways surprisingly like such mundane activities. Like sleeping or grooming it is easy to do and quickly becomes automatic or habitual. Like eating, it is ritually flexible. Just as dinner can range from a quick and simple solitary affair to a decorous feast, so Evening Prayer can be accomplished in seven minutes by an individual in a hurry or by a hundred people singing an elaborate Evensong that takes an hour and a half. These activities "feel" very different in some ways, but just as the nutritional benefit of the quick repast and the fancy feast may be identical, so may the spiritual nourishment of the two different forms of Evening Prayer. On a given day the same psalms, lessons, canticles, and collects will be read (or sung), and the invariable—in traditional liturgical language, the "ordinary"—elements always remain the same, so the two services have exactly the same content. They are simply "packaged" in diametrically different ways.

The Daily Office is, in fact, the "Common Prayer" referred to in the title of the *Book of Common Prayer* and every preceding prayer book. All other services mentioned above fall under the second heading, "Sacraments and Other Rites and Ceremonies and Their Administration." Although baptism, special liturgies, Eucharist, pastoral and episcopal services all are corporate, they are in a basic sense not common. They are differentiated by task or service. Various Orders preside over them, and they are arranged in ordered ways. The Orders perform their liturgical ministries for the rest of the church, like waiters,[2] cooks, and custodians at a restaurant. The Office alone is led by any person, "clerical or lay," as the first rubric in the *Book of Common Prayer* states (p. 140).[3]

Of course, the Office is "led" only when more than one person participates. The Office may be read by an individual or by a group—unlike the other services in the *Book of Common Prayer*, which, like the Eucharist, must be prayed in a group context. The Office, in its origins, is a hybrid of private devotions and public services, and partakes of both. There are advantages to group prayer; there are also and equally advantages to solitary use of the Daily Office. As presented in the prayer book, the Office does assume a group context. Certain small modifications are therefore helpful, as we shall see, when using the Office for individual devotions. Either setting, however, has virtues. Even when we pray in group context, the Office conveys a privacy and a personal aspect lacking in the more public forms. When we pray in solitude, on the other hand, the Office communicates by its very form and content that others, although not physically present, are using the same format. Thus the isolation of praying in solitude and the impersonality of praying in a group are avoided.

Characteristics of the Daily Office

At this point, it should be clear that the Daily Office has strengths that lend it its essential character and distinguish it from other liturgical and devotional practices.

1. The Office is *daily*. Theoretically, it can be repeated every day and, like other daily activities mentioned above, it is somewhat ordinary or mundane by nature. For this reason, it often strikes nonpractitioners as prosaic and boring, routine and mechanical. Most of these words seem less than attractive, but they characterize most if not all daily activities. To paraphrase T. S. Eliot,

humankind can bear only so much of the extraordinary. The Office's opposite in this respect is the occasional service, such as Good Friday, which may occur only once a year, or the pastoral service such as baptism, which may only occur once in a lifetime.

2. The Office is *brief*. All daily tasks are, by definition, "brief." Read by an individual, the Office of Morning Prayer, complete with two readings, canticles, psalmody, three collects, free intercessions, and silences after the readings, takes on the average about ten minutes. It thus can fit into most morning routines: most people spend a similar amount of time reading the newspaper, eating breakfast, or getting dressed. In this the Office contrasts especially with elaborate rites such as the Easter Vigil, the Great Litany, or Tenebrae. The length of these services provides part of their meaning.

3. The Office is *stable*. That is, it does not vary much from day to day. A brief Office could be followed the next day by an equally brief but totally different order of prayer, but that would violate this principle of stability. This principle, I realize, runs counter to notions many of us entertain about our need for diversity and variety—but an honest examination of daily routines will for most of us reveal a great deal of stable activity. The Eucharist is, by comparison, hugely variable. Monday's Eucharist (if there is one) might be almost unrecognizable in comparison to Sunday's.

4. The Office is, conversely, *flexible*. In his Rule, one of the earliest guides to communal Christian living, Basil the Great sets times for prayer and psalms—the raw materials of the Daily Office. Then he adds this principle of flexibility: "I think that variety and diversity in the prayers and psalms recited at appointed hours are desirable for the reason that routine and boredom, somehow, often cause distraction in the soul, while by change and variety it is enriched in devotion and renewed in sobriety."[4] Our Daily Office incorporates this sensible principle. It is very brief in basic form, but can be enriched and expanded almost without limit. Thus many spend a half-hour daily at Morning Prayer. The Office is also flexible in its simplicity—it needs no special equipment or location, but can also be prayed in an elaborate liturgical context. And though it can be said by individuals, it is equally appropriate for small or very large groups. It can be said in private homes or public

places, in small chapels, large cathedrals, outdoors, anywhere. Indeed, one of the Office's virtues is that none of these settings is "best." Each provides a valid, but different, experience. In this aspect the Office contrasts especially with solemnities such as Ash Wednesday, in which the same lessons, prayers, and structure recur every year.

5. The Office is *incremental* and *sequential*. Praying it daily means participating in a sequence; every day, something new is added. This applies above all to the lectionary. The daily lessons from Scripture are read in a sequence, "in course," and not in arbitrary order. On any given day, the readings begin where the previous day's readings ended. This is a natural approach to reading; it is the way one approaches a long book, for example. In this incremental aspect, the Office is almost in a category by itself. Only the weekly Eucharist could be said to have a similar incremental pattern of readings.

6. The Office is *nonhierarchical*. Hieros is the Greek word for priest, and therefore this word will serve our purposes as well as any. No Order has any prerogatives within the Daily Office. The rubric on page 36 of the *Book of Common Prayer* (citations in text appear henceforth as *BCP*, with the page number) suggests it well: "The term 'Officiant' is used to designate the person, clerical or lay, who leads the Office." Only the bishop has any prerogatives within the Daily Office, and that is merely to pronounce a blessing at the end, not to officiate. In other words, like monasticism, which contributed a great deal to its development, the Daily Office began as a movement in which laity were equal to clergy in leadership and responsibility. In this, the Office contrasts strongly with the Eucharist and other sacramental rites, all of which are normally—although not rigidly—organized according to Order. We could have labeled the Office "lay-centered," but that might imply the exclusion of clergy or suggest that the Office is not useful for clergy. The Office stands alone in not being differentiated by hierarchy.

7. The Office may be *corporate*. It can be read privately, but when anyone else is present they should be invited to participate. The Office is supposed to be shared. Again, the rubric is helpful. If anyone else is present, "it is appropriate" that s/he be assigned the lessons, for example. Even when read by the individual, that many

others are reading the same Office (with variations as noted) and the same lections should reinforce this shared, communal sense.

8. Finally, the Daily Office is *comprehensive*. It encourages a reading of the entirety of Scripture and can encompass more. It encourages observance of the Christian week, month, and year. It allows for the widest possible variety of intercessory expression, including prayers from every century and encouraging free petitions. It allows musical expression of an almost unlimited nature, or silences of whatever duration is desired. Most important, perhaps, it spans the length and breadth of the spiritual life. The Office is appropriate. More than appropriate, it is strengthening and comforting on occasions of joy, sorrow, grief, calm, confusion, boredom, elation, exultation, temptation, and victory.

These eight principles balance the Daily Office and give it its strength. They are by no means "rules," for we violate them regularly. The Evensong mentioned above clearly cannot be characterized as "brief." The quick reading of Evening Prayer, omitting everything but essentials, can hardly be called "comprehensive." The individual who always prays the Office in private will find it difficult to realize the corporate aspect, although it is always there. Any given feast day breaks the incremental and sequential principle by interrupting the readings and the repetition of the week's collect.

These are, however, the characteristics that make the Office what it is. Anyone who prays the Office regularly for any length of time will discover the principles almost instinctively, for they are built into its structure and content. Whenever the Office has languished, or been forgotten or misused, we find that one or more of these virtues have been lost.

CHAPTER ONE

A Brief History
of the Daily Office

One day at three in the afternoon, the hour of prayer,
Peter and John were on their way up to the temple.
—Acts 3:1

The word *office* is made up of two Latin words: *opus*, meaning "work," and *facere*, meaning "to do." Thus the word *office* means "to do work." Our ordinary uses of the word thus make sense. Someone goes "to the office" for work or exercises "an office" with responsibilities. "Officials" are workers with authority and responsibility for service. These are the denotations of the word. Its connotations, such as seriousness, severity, and laboriousness, are congruent. The Latin word *officium* was used to mean "duty," as in ethical and moral behavior: a colloquial rendering would be "what you're supposed to do." Thus Cicero's comprehensive treatise on "how to behave" is called *De officia*.

In theological language, we use the word *office* to identify the specific, short, nonsacramental services of prayer, readings, and perhaps meditations, which are offered much more frequently than the sacramental services. The etymology we have just examined makes *office* practically a Latin equivalent for the word *liturgy*, which means "people's work" in Greek. But these words are distinguished from one another in English: "liturgy" means, rather, any corporate service of the church, sacramental or otherwise, whereas office can refer to a noncorporate service—an individual devotion.

Jewish practice at the time of Jesus involved all sorts of ritual possibilities. We know of four different types of worship that were practiced regularly. First was temple worship, with its detailed round of sacrifices and offerings. Second, synagogue worship was practiced several times each day by a public congregation of adult intercessors and inquirers. Third, family services, with their unique blend of readings, praises, and blessings over food and beverage, were observed every week. Fourth, individuals prayed

1

private devotions, characterized by brief prayers, psalms, and scriptural quotations.

All of these services were offered at specific times. But of the four, temple services and, to an extent, family services were of the *kairos* sort we defined in the previous chapter. Synagogue and private devotions and, to some extent, family services, were *chronos* events. Synagogue services took place several times during the week, and daily in some areas; family services took place daily, with special occasions such as the eve or beginning of the Sabbath occurring weekly; individual devotions took place two to four times a day, every day.[1]

Liturgical scholars have puzzled over the relation and line of descent among these practices and the Daily Office. Unfortunately, evidence for the transition is weak since we know little about Christian worship of a nonsacramental nature in the earliest centuries of the church. We know that the earliest Christians prayed a daily nonsacramental prayer, but this was apparently an oral tradition for some centuries.

We do know that when the Daily Office first appeared in written form, in the fourth century, it was already fully developed. It looked very much like the Office in the current prayer book, and bore strong signs of influence from two of the Jewish services—synagogue and private devotions. The other two services, temple and family worship, seem to have influenced the Eucharist. The fourth-century Office resembled synagogue services in its mixture of prayer, psalm, and reading, and resembled private devotions in its frequency and suitability for individuals. At the same time, we should recognize that any of the four worship traditions could have influenced the Daily Office and the Eucharist.

What were the two services that influenced our Office like? *Private devotions* were to be taken seriously by the devout and observant Jew—as seriously as sin offerings in the Temple—but for different reasons. Various Old Testament[2] passages such as Psalm 119:164—"seven times a day do I praise you"—enjoined the individual believer to pray several times daily. The verse later was used to explain the sevenfold monastic Office that came to inform monastic practice.[3] Three times a day in the majority of places, Jews prayed privately upon arising or early in the morning, at midday, and at nightfall. The devotions took the form of psalms appropriate to these occasions, brief scriptural excerpts, short set prayers, and sometimes the brief "Creed" of the traditional Jew, the *Shema'*, "Hear, O Israel…"

A consideration of *synagogue devotions* can begin by stating that *synagogue* is the Greek word for "assembly." The synagogue's origins are again tantalizingly obscure and debatable. The question of whether the synagogue arose in reaction mainly to exile, to the destruction of the Temple, or simply as a complement to temple services—or as a combination of all three causes—has never been answered satisfactorily. But it is clear that, from ancient times to the present, the synagogue service has resembled the service of individual devotions—consisting of readings, psalms, and prayers—in a more elaborate version.

The question of which came first, synagogue or private devotion, also cannot be answered. We do know that the earliest Christians mentioned—the apostolic Christians in the New Testament—seem to have practiced both, as no doubt Jesus did himself. Jesus frequently taught in the synagogue at times of gathering. Paul did the same. Peter and John went to the Temple during the afternoon hour of prayer (Acts 3). Jesus similarly was often seen in solitary prayer, and in Matthew 6 he commends private prayer behind a closed door.

Devout, practicing Jews such as Jesus' disciples were enriched by this daily prayer, which included not only petitions but also daily readings in the Scriptures. Paul was well trained in the rabbinical tradition, but what of the other New Testament writers? No matter what theories of authorship we accept, no one but Paul seems to have had access to that sort of intellectual and theological training. Yet the New Testament is replete with theology and saturated with scriptural (Old Testament) references throughout. This is understandable if such references are partly the product of a tradition of private and synagogue worship that offered daily scriptural readings. This practice is probably the best way of assimilating a rich tradition.

The early generations of Christians continued the practice of private prayer, developing it along Christian lines but keeping the basic elements. We know from various letters, manuals of discipline, and other writings from the first Christian centuries that they kept the threefold daily observance, using cycles of scriptural readings and psalms and the Lord's Prayer. Some practiced this observance in synagogue-like groups, groups of friends, or family gatherings, and others individually; probably, as in Judaism, the type of service depended on the circumstances. The *Apostolic Tradition*, for example, a second-century document that includes an outline for eucharistic prayer, mentions a daily Morning Office based on Psalter and lections, complete with brief instruction, which all Christians are encouraged to attend. At the same time, of course, the church kept and developed the two primary sacraments of baptism and Eucharist, but the evidence confirms that these were *kairos* elements: the church used the Eucharist to mark the week, festive days, and special occasions. A daily form of devotion marked chronological time.

By the fourth century, these practices had taken on two forms that scholars label the *cathedral* and *monastic* versions of the Daily Office. The first label is a little misleading, in that the version was not exclusive to cathedral churches but was the form used in various parishes and other groupings of ordinary Christians. Over the years, however, it became more elaborate, and therefore more of a public liturgical event and less suitable for individual use. This may be the reason it began to appear in written form. Larger groups need written forms to keep order. Development of the cathedral version also meant the loss of one of the key virtues of the Office, that of flexibility.

The monastic version began to develop with the proliferation of the monastic movement, again a product of the fourth century. During the first twenty-five years of that era, Christianity went from a persecuted to an officially approved cult when Constantine legitimized the faith that he believed had led him to material and military success. That proved to be a decidedly mixed blessing. The faith was now safe, and could bring material benefits, but for many serious Christians it seemed to have gone soft and to have compromised with the secular world it formerly had challenged. Christianity was losing its edge.

Many ardent souls retreated to the monastic fringes and created the first "alternative church" and alternative lifestyle. Living in more or less ordered family- or military-style communities, they practiced communal living, charity, moderate to heroic austerity—and lives of constant prayer. They expanded the two-, three-, or fourfold daily round of prayer to six, seven, or eight Offices spread throughout the day and sometimes well into the night. Like most other Christian groups, they celebrated the Eucharist weekly, but the Office was theirs, and they tailored it to suit their chronological arrangement. Thus they contributed enormously to the Office's enrichment, flexibility, and development.

What was added? This is an important question, for it enables us to separate the essential elements of the Office from the *optional*. We shall discuss every facet of the Office in chapter 2, but we can briefly chart its development here. Various formal *opening rites* were introduced. Monks included a *confession* as an opening rite for certain Offices. *Antiphons* were composed from Scripture to frame Psalms, and *canticles*—"short songs"—were invented for use between lessons. The *Apostles' Creed* began to be used as part of the Office in many contexts. *Collects* were introduced early, at first as a single collect to summarize the theme of the day, then as three collects in the Western monasteries, and finally as multiple collects amounting simply to an accumulation of prayers (see below, "The Collect"). Various *concluding rites* were added and also became fixed and formalized. Finally, parallel elaboration occurred in *music*, as traditional settings for the Office developed in the leisure of the monastic environment.

These were the basic elaborations in form. Their contribution to the life of the Daily Office was to enrich it and to add to its flexibility. The negative aspect was twofold: these additions worked against the principle of brevity, and soon came to be understood as essential rather than optional, thus working against flexibility. This made no difference to the monks, who were striving to spend their days in prayer, nor to the clergy, increasingly understood as a professional class similarly divorced from secular life. But for anyone else the elaborated service became increasingly exclusive, simply because no one else had the time to spend in prayer. The early Office might be prayed in fifteen minutes even in a group setting; the elaborated Office took at least a half hour.

A second change occurred within the lectionary. As noted, the classic idea for the Office lectionary was the sequential, incremental reading of Scripture: the individual or group began a new day's reading where yesterday's had ended. This provided continuity from day to day and assured a rational, comprehensive experience of Scripture. Naturally, the sequence would be broken for special days and seasons, such as Easter Week and the newly developing observance of the nativity, but even then the lessons conformed to a minisequence rather than being idiosyncratic and sporadic.

The exception was the individual commemoration. As early as the apostolic era—roughly the first one hundred years of the common era—local communities began to set aside anniversary dates for their great martyrs and exemplars, which is the origin of the Saints' Days. For these days, the sequential reading was suspended and lections appropriate to the life and witness of the commemorated Christian were substituted. But these interruptions were by definition exceptional.

This sort of observance proved enormously popular, however, and a gradual proliferation of holy days occurred over several centuries. By the later Middle Ages there were many more days of special observance than "ordinary days." Naturally, this destroyed the sense of sequential readings. Flexibility and variety had displaced stability. The content for the Daily Office became a bewildering daily tribute to a cavalcade of saints, rather than a patient trek through Scripture for its own sake as the Word of God.

The Daily Office, in taking these two directions, was being distanced from the secular Christian person. In cathedral practice, the Office increasingly came to be seen as the domain of the clergy. On the other hand, the monastic movement was, and still is, essentially a lay movement. Therefore, its appropriation of the Office was more congruent with the Office's nature. But though monasticism is lay-based, it demands a distinct type of layperson. One must be free and willing to sever all human and community ties in order to affiliate with the new family and community. By definition, the monastic life is not for everybody. Neither were its Offices. Few people in the secular world, including secular deacons and bishops, had the opportunity to break seven or more times for daily prayer, however briefly. Only those with leisure could do so, and private prayers for the privileged were hardly the idea that monastics intended to promulgate.

In other words, while the forms of the Office had expanded, its usage had diminished. Among the first generations of Christians, everyone performed daily prayer whether alone or in groups, a practice that must have contributed enormous benefits in terms of solidarity and catechetical formation. A young person growing up in a Christian family in 150 C.E. would have been exposed to an atmosphere in which everyone read psalms, said certain prayers, made certain faith affirmations, and savored Holy Scripture every day. A child growing up in a Christian family in the year 375 would have known the property of an established church, seen magnificent services and lovely mosaic depictions of saints, and heard rich liturgical music—all impossible in earlier centuries. But she would have known of the Daily Office as something "done" in cathedrals and bigger parishes "by" bishops and priests,[4] and by monks in their remote communities. She would not have seen mother, father, brother, and sister reading Scripture to one another or repeating the week's prayer concerns morning and night.

The daily reading schedule was similarly altered during this later patristic period. The observance of Saints' Days, a sporadic event in the earliest church, through the centuries gradually came to dominate the calendar. Thus the sequence of readings was constantly being broken—to the point that, more often than not, the biblical readings for any given day were relevant, albeit tentatively, only to the saint being commemorated. The ideal of reading through Scripture book by book was lost. In general, it stands to reason that stability and flexibility are in mutual tension: when either becomes too dominant, the other is sacrificed. This resembles the classic tension in any art between repetition and variation. Too much repetition results in mechanistic boredom, too much variety results in chaos. The Office, as the Middle Ages waned, was becoming confused and unwieldy.

Thus several of the Office's key features were sacrificed: its corporate nature, nonhierarchical quality, brevity, stability, and sequential principle for readings. It was daily, as always, and more flexible than ever before, but its distinctive character had clearly been lost. Any service that takes up to an hour every day necessarily becomes the work of specialists within the church—monks and clergy. The laity cannot "own" such a service.

The need for a more truly catholic Office, a form for daily prayer that could have widespread use within the church, did not pass away. The lay origins of the Office may have been forgotten, but knowledgeable and serious laypeople nevertheless felt the lack of a daily devotional form. They felt the impulse to "borrow" from the monasteries what seemed an exclusively monastic practice, as though monastics had invented the Office rather than simply adapting it for their particular needs. In response to the desires of serious secular Christians, various primers and breviaries began to be compiled. These were nothing but abbreviated forms of the embellished Office. They restored the brevity of the classic Office; indeed, they unintentionally re-created aspects of the classic Office. Nothing produced around 1400 looks as much like the early Office as the lay primer or breviary. Because, however, primers and breviaries retained the developed lectionary and used various embellishments indiscriminately, they did not restore the virtues of stability and sequential lections.

They proved enormously popular, however. By the fifteenth century, they were among the most frequently produced books in the world, the last popular product of the pre-Gutenberg era. Wealthy laypersons commissioned or otherwise procured richly decorated texts called "books of hours," some of which are extant today and valued primarily as art objects.[5] In their very opulence, however, such works exhibit an exclusivity that worked against the corporate nature of the Office. Only the very wealthy could afford to have them, and because the liturgies they contained were still rather embellished—though not nearly as embellished as the forms used by monks—their usage was further restricted to the wealthy, who had time to spare. In the later medieval era, this often meant rich women whose husbands were busy with the knightly responsibilities of management and defense.

Compounding these difficulties was the simple issue of language, an issue that in part precipitated the Reformation. Like all other forms of worship in the West, the Office—whether in breviary, monastic, or cathedral form—was in Latin. This was a language that, curiously, originally had replaced Greek, the "vulgar" tongue, as the language of the majority in the late Roman Empire and early Middle Ages. But by the year 1300, Latin had become a specialized language understood only by the highly educated, and used by virtually no one.

The Reformation of the sixteenth century brought several reactions. Many Reformed bodies simply dismissed the idea of a Daily Office as impossibly corrupt, and suggested impromptu, informal daily devotions for their members. This is perhaps the classic "Protestant" response. Others, such as the Lutherans, worked out reformed Offices and daily devotional patterns, essentially trying to restore the earlier character of the Office. The Roman Catholic liturgical reformer, Cardinal Quinones, tried the same approach within the Roman church, but the more successful, and dominant, Roman tendency was to embrace the late-medieval embellished Office with all its features.

Thomas Cranmer and his circle, which led the unique Anglican approach to reform, determined to restore the Daily Office to its rightful status and utility as a daily practice for as many members of the church as possible. Using both Luther's experiments and Quinones's revisions, Cranmer compiled several successive prayer books featuring a newly simplified Office with a restored sequential lectionary, in the "common tongue" of the people. The result was the *Book of Common Prayer* of 1549. This work, and all editions to the present day, opens with the Daily Office in the English language.

Cranmer's Office restored most of the classic features of Office liturgy. It was brief: Cranmer combined the sevenfold monastic services into two, making various elements optional. The resulting service began to conform to our classic principles. It was stable: there was very little change in form from day to day. It was incremental: Cranmer worked out a rich yearlong lectionary that went through the Old Testament and the New Testament twice. It was flexible, although not nearly as various as the Office had become in the five centuries preceding Cranmer's work.

To what extent the revised Office was corporate and nonhierarchical is debatable. Cranmer clearly envisioned—and stipulated—an Office read in church, meaning "at church" and nowhere else. Early editions of the *Book of Common Prayer* specified this fact. Clergy were clearly needed to lead the Office, and a presbyter or priest was normally to be officiant. In the first edition, all clergy connected with a parish were required to read the Office there, publicly, every day. In the second edition of the prayer book, they were required to read the Office daily whether attached to a parish or not. This seems a small distinction, but suggests a widely divergent understanding of the Office. In the first case, the understanding is of a service provided by the clergy for the corporate life of the church; the second version turns the Office into a service essentially for the clergy, into a private, clerical discipline detached from corporate life. Cranmer at first envisioned a church wherein the Office was said publicly every day, and was attended by parishioners from the neighborhood. Later, perhaps guessing that this gathering was unlikely, he guaranteed the survival of the Office and the edification of the clergy by reverting to the medieval ideal of the Office as clerical discipline.

Almost to the present, that understanding of the Office has prevailed within Anglicanism, as generations of clergy understood it as their private daily responsibility to "say" the Office. This idea has intrinsic value. Few would find the daily discipline of prayer and study for clergy anything but desirable. Its weakness in our understanding is that it clericalizes or sacerdotalizes the Office. It fails to guarantee the corporate and nonclerical nature of daily Morning and Evening Prayer. Quite the opposite: it virtually guarantees that the Office will be understood as something "for priests."

Very recently, the requirement that clergy "say" the Office daily has been rescinded in many parts of the Anglican communion. The reason is not to slacken the discipline of clergy, but to encourage a broader and wider use of the Daily Office—to encourage laity and the other Orders to use it.[6] Instead, what has resulted in many places is a virtual eclipse of the Office, with no one using it.

The current American prayer book presents a revised Office, deliberately intended to be the property of the entire church. Historically, this amounts to a completion of the work of Cranmer. He envisioned an Office said daily "in church" and attended by all Orders; the current *Book of Common Prayer*, realizing that that may prove impossible in the majority of parishes and for the majority of baptized persons, instead presents an Office that can be prayed by anyone, anywhere. It retains some corporate character. In some ways the Office works better when two or three gather than when only one person is present. But otherwise, it is portable and nonclerical—the officiant may be lay, bishop, priest, or deacon, and no mention is made of location.

The Office in many ways thus has come full circle historically. It began, in the formative years of the undivided church, as a form of prayer that was stable, brief, flexible, sequential, nonclerical, corporate, daily, and comprehensive. It gradually lost most of these characteristics, becoming elaborate, rigid, and clericalized. And then, through a series of reforms, it regained its original character. For several centuries, it has been stable, brief, flexible, and sequential. Only recently has it also become nonclerical and comprehensive—which may warn us about our tendency toward sacerdotalization. Many individuals and groups have discovered the Office or are in the process of that discovery; it is for them, in part, that this book is written. Significantly, these individuals and groups include priests, but also laypersons, deacons, and bishops. The Office is for everyone in the same way that eating and sleeping are for everyone, not for priests alone.

Finally, history has given the Daily Office one additional peculiarity with some negative aspects. As we have seen, the Office is both public and private. It is spiritually amphibious. At various times, one of these aspects has been stressed, often to the virtual exclusion of the other. In its immediate post-Reformation history, the Office seems to have been thought of as primarily a public rite: it was short, simple, and everyday, but the expectation was that it would be prayed "in church," that is, within the local parish building. In seventeenth-century England, where the overwhelming majority was not only Christian but also belonged to the national church, it was not an unreasonable expectation that many would avail themselves of the opportunity and attend before and after their workday.

Later, and especially in nations where the church was not established and the Office increasingly became the property of the clergy, the private aspect was stressed. The Office was thought of primarily as a private devotion, performed by priests and bishops, seminarians, and extremely devout laypersons. Parish priests felt obligated to say their Office, much as monks were obligated to say the hours of the breviary, whether they were in church or not. Unlike the monk, however, who always knew that the rest of the monastic community was keeping the Office that he was saying privately, the priest could develop a sense that he was carrying the Office with him. When he read it at the rectory, in a carriage, or on a country walk, he knew very well that it was not being prayed in his parish simultaneously.

The dual aspect—the amphibious nature of the Office—was never entirely lost, as all previous editions of the *Book of Common Prayer* suggest. Any parish, indeed any community, was always free to pray it on a regular basis if it so desired, and any individual has always been free to read it privately if he or she was interested. It remains fair to say, however, that at various times this amphibious quality has not been well understood by many within the church, and certainly never very well publicized.

CHAPTER TWO

The Shape of the Office as Instructed Morning Prayer

This is the day on which the Lord has acted: let us exult and rejoice in it.
—Psalm 118:24

In this chapter I will attempt to present a practical analysis of the Office, geared toward those interested in praying the Office rather than studying it academically. In my experience, understanding the elements that constitute the Office helps in two ways. First, it helps an officiant, committee, or individual praying the Office to choose among the options provided. For example, there is an optional confession near the beginning of the Office (*BCP* 79), and some seasonal sentences before that (*BCP* 75). Yet the first required element is the phrase "Lord, open our lips" (*BCP* 80). Some gentle and informed guidelines can help choose among these elements on any occasion and in any season. In general, the flexibility of the current Office, so valuable in itself, can lead to confusion. Guidelines—not hard rules, but gentle principles of direction—can mitigate that confusion.

Second, and even more important, understanding the elements of a service of worship enhances the praying of it. Put colloquially, knowing what something is supposed to be helps make it what it is supposed to be. Put psychologically, we might say that the cognitive aspect reinforces the conative. During the Eucharist, for example, knowing that the Eucharistic Prayer is intended to be a prayer of praise and thanksgiving helps participants to hear and to pray it that way. Countless inquirers have discovered this aspect of the prayer through confirmation classes and "instructed Eucharists." This simple knowledge lends an intentionality to worship that is otherwise largely missing. The same holds true for the Office: knowing what the canticle is supposed to contribute helps it make that contribution.

Without such understanding, worship tends to be a jumble of religious-sounding phrases and frenetic page turning.[1] Few would

want to pray in such a way daily, or even weekly. Most intuit that
something fundamentally wrong must be taking place. For when
worship is poorly understood it tends to degenerate into supersti-
tion and magic, cult degenerating into occult.[2] My purpose
throughout is to present the Office as a practical, accessible mode
of prayer. Knowing the shape of the Office and its constituent elements is valuable if it helps us to do that.

In the pages that follow I will describe each element, touch on
its history, and define its function. Then I outline the combination
of options that has worked for me and for parishes with which I
have been associated. In no case is this material meant to be pre-
scriptive; it is merely suggestive. Every individual or group praying
the Office should work out their own system. I simply list what I
have found useful by way of illustrating this very principle.

Throughout this chapter, the paradigmatic example will be
Morning Prayer. The general principles apply equally to Evening
Prayer, the Noonday Office, Compline, individual devotions, and
Rite One, but I will speak of Morning Prayer for two reasons.
First, Morning Prayer is the initial "event" in the prayer book, the
more familiar Office, and also the richest in terms of options. The
greatest selection of canticles, for example, is provided with
Morning Prayer.

Second, Morning Prayer is in many ways the norm for all the
Offices. The themes of rebirth and renewal, forgiveness and rec-
onciliation, catechesis and covenant contained within the Morning
Office tend to make it the quintessential form for daily devotion.
And, as we shall see in a discussion of the theology of the Office,
these themes make it an extension of, and complement to, the primary sacraments of baptism and Eucharist. Theologically, then,
the other Offices, beginning with Evening Prayer, while exhibiting
in each case a distinctive tone and texture, replicate the essential
shape and content of Morning Prayer.

That shape is probably the most obvious factor that versions of
the Office have in common. I use the word *shape* to recall an essential study of the Eucharist, *The Shape of the Liturgy*, by Dom Gregory
Dix.[3] Dix's work traces the history of the Mass and offers a moving
appreciation of its meaning, but its central idea is that the
Eucharist has a classic shape that lends it character and strength.

That shape has persisted through centuries of experience, elaboration, and experimentation.

The same holds true for the Daily Office. It too has a shape discernible throughout its various manifestations in Morning Prayer, Evening Prayer, the Noonday Office, Compline, devotions for individuals, and their various embellishments. Through the centuries, despite the historical steps and missteps we traced in chapter 1, that shape has remained remarkably distinct.

When we approach the Office by discussing its shape, we approach at a distance as we might a great painting for the first time, attempting to discern its outlines, its strongest features, its overall pattern and impression. Later, we can step closer and explore the smaller features: patterns within patterns, texture, brushwork.

What we discover when we "stand back" from the Office is simply that the Daily Office is tripartite. The prayer book labels each of the three parts in large type: "The Invitatory and Psalter" (*BCP* 80); "The Lessons" (*BCP* 84); and "The Prayers" (*BCP* 97). The Eucharist, by contrast, is larger than the Office, but has two parts. It comprises the liturgy of the Word ("The Word of God," *BCP* 355) and the liturgy of the Table ("The Holy Communion," *BCP* 361 and elsewhere). The services are similar in that each part has a distinct function, form, and feeling. The three parts of the Daily Office, in fact, are like the three movements of a sonata in music, or a triptych in art: they add up to a single spiritual experience, but each stands in contrast to the other.

The first part—the first "movement" of the Office—centers in the psalm appointed for the occasion, and its mode is praise. The Psalms, as we shall see, express an extraordinary scope of human emotion, but their primary note is praise. That is why the collection ends with the exuberant praise songs in Psalms 144 through 150. The fixed psalm—Psalm 95, Psalm 100, or the canticle *Pascha nostrum* during the Great Fifty Days—is invariably a praise song. So the opening mode of the Office is always positive, refreshing, and upbeat, like the sprightly or energetic first movement of a sonata. For those who pray the Morning Prayer, then, every day begins on the affirmative note of praise of God.[4]

The second part—the second movement—is centered in the readings. It is thus slower, deliberate, and thoughtful—again, like

the second movement of many sonatas. This is the most widely varied part of the Office, since the readings change from season to season and from day to day. They encompass almost the entirety of Holy
Scripture, the Apocrypha included. We are thereby reminded of
God's acts in the past. The readings are, technically, a kind of anamnesis, a "ceasing to forget" the mighty acts of God. This is the "daily
bread" portion of the Office, wherein we hear God's Word daily,
allowing it to inform and reform us. Because we hear it sequentially,
moreover, we begin to experience a continuity in our reading from
one day to the next—an extremely important aspect of the dynamic.

The third movement centers in the petitions. This part is often
energetic and passionate—once again, roughly comparable to the
third movement of many sonatas. Its content is what many people
assume to be the whole of prayer, which is making requests of
God. The third portion of the Office gives us scope for making
requests, but puts the activity in its place—a tertiary place—and
structures it so as to give the requests the greatest possible meaning. This portion of the Office gives us a voice for prayer. It supports
our own petitions by putting them in the context of the requests
that humankind for many millennia has directed toward God.

It is important to notice a simple but meaningful dynamic
among the three movements. In part 1, we address God. In part 2,
we listen to God. In part 3, we address God again. To some extent
this mirrors the dynamic of the collect, which can also be seen as
the Office in microcosm. But more importantly, this simple alternation reinforces the sense of the Office as a dialogue between two
parties in which the central event is not our word directed toward
God, but our listening to God's Word directed toward us.

As we have said, this shape is common to all versions of the
Office in the prayer book—Morning Prayer, Evening Prayer, and
the various minor Offices.[5] These versions exhibit an idiosyncratic,
unmistakable character, a tone and set of themes perfectly
matched to time and purpose. For the Daily Office, more than any
other rite or order in the prayer book, is geared to time in all the
ways we mark and understand it—to time of day, to day of week
and month, and to season. It distinguishes not only between
chronos and *kairos*, but among the ways we subdivide both. And
that distinguishing process begins with Morning Prayer.

Morning has certain inevitable and natural associations for humankind. It suggests freshness, beauty, and purity. We say "pure as the morning dew" and "handsome as the dawn." Homer sang of dawn approaching with "rosy fingers," an image that became indelible in the Western imagination. Morning recalls the mind to origins and beginnings, to the mysteries of time and space. At dawn, the appearance of everything changes, and we respond at a deep level. Jesus himself compares the experience of entering the last age to "waking from sleep." More rationally, morning also represents opportunity, a beginning, and, by implication, forgiveness: a new day brings new opportunities or second chances. We say that one must get up "early in the morning" to fool a clever person. We associate morning with urgency, with reality, with happenings. Finally, morning is associated with the possibility of the triumph of life over death. Virtually every great faith has understood sleep as a "likeness" of death, as seventeenth-century poet John Donne wrote, and waking, therefore, as a perfect symbol of immortality.

The morning has, also, a primacy in Christian tradition. Christianity is a "morning" faith. This is true primarily because, in biblical history, morning has two preeminent associations: creation and resurrection. The first day of creation seems to suggest morning. Yahweh creates light first of all, and to us that says "morning." Throughout Scripture, then, the natural associations mentioned above are reinforced with theological weight, as significant characters rise early in the morning to do significant things. Abraham rises early in the morning for his test of faith with Isaac. Moses ascends Mount Sinai early in the morning to receive the tablets of the Law. Finally, for the Christian reader, biblical theology and tradition achieve their climax on the paschal morning, when Christ rises from the dead and the reality of the new life dawns on the disciples and witnesses. For this reason, morning for the Christian is itself paradigmatic. It is the time that most naturally symbolizes the central tenet of Christian faith. Morning, to use the language of the religious philosopher Rudolph Otto, is "numinous" time.

All this background provides a subtext for Morning Prayer. Unlike Evening Prayer, which, as we shall see, strongly expresses a consciousness of time of day, Morning Prayer subordinates the theme of morning to the great themes of Christian theology and tradition. But since, as just noted, these themes are in perfect harmony with the connotations of morning, it becomes difficult to separate one from the other. The emotions in which the entire Office centers—praise, recollection, petitions for the future—are synchronous with these larger connotations and morning events of the past. Throughout the Office is a powerful undercurrent of praising, knowing, and beseeching of the God "whose light divides the day from the night, and turns the shadow of death into morning" (*BCP* 99, "Collect for the Renewal of Life").

Opening Rites

Having discerned the shape of the Office we may now approach closer and investigate its constituent elements in detail. For the Office is also a conversation with this God—an encounter, through words and silence and physical presence, with a conscious and living Other. Therefore, psychological and even sociopolitical "rules" apply. When we answer the telephone or the door, when we meet others by chance in the workplace or the street, when we first encounter family or friends in the morning, we feel the need for form. We use formal greetings. We do not simply "start talking." We do not abruptly bring up urgent concerns, pressing matters, exciting news, the latest joke. We feel the need, as we say colloquially, to "break the ice." The same holds for worship in general, and for the particular conversation that is the Daily Office. While there is nothing stopping us from cracking open Psalm books and reading together, this would seem awkward and strange. Nothing stops us, furthermore, from presenting God with a lists of desires and complaints—in emergencies, that is exactly what we should do.[6] That is not, however, the way Jesus taught us to pray, and the Daily Office is not, normally, a matter of emergency. Therefore opening rites have developed for the Office: simple, brief, but definite ways of opening prayer.

Note that I use the term "ways," not "way." The opening rite was fixed and invariable in almost every previous version of the *Book of Common Prayer*, but no longer. The flexible nature of the prayer-book Office is now clear from the very start, where we have three options for beginning. We may start with the appropriate seasonal sentence (*BCP* 75–78), with the sentence plus an act of confession (*BCP* 79), or with the versicle "Lord, open our lips" (*BCP* 80). How do we choose? What is the function of each?

In many ways, the Office is a palimpsest of worship, including traces of practices tested through the centuries. We have a striking example at the outset. The most ancient way of opening the Office is the *versicle*, "Lord, open our lips," based on Psalm 51.[7] The idea was to break the verbal fast of the night by making these the first words we say in the morning; that idea was practiced literally in monasteries. This verse opens Morning Prayer in the earliest extant versions of the Office.

It is a simple and striking way to begin the Office, and it sets the prevalent theological tone of triumphal paschal joy and praise. In its small way, by virtue of its age and meaning, this versicle is the equivalent of the theological theme of *Christus Victor*—an idea we will explore in more detail in a discussion of the theology of the Office (see chapter 5). It should be used often as the simplest way of opening the Office. Those praying the Office individually may find it helpful to substitute the singular pronoun, as in "Lord, open *my* lips," rather than carrying on a pseudodialogue. This sort of commonsense alteration of texts is always to be encouraged.

The *seasonal sentence* may be used with the versicle. It is required when using the confession. Its usefulness is fairly obvious in calling to mind the seasonal context. This may sound simplistic, but it really is not. Our church takes the Christian year very seriously, realizing that we as human beings respond to a sense of season. There are also sentences provided for Saints' Days and occasions of thanksgiving, and several sentences appropriate "at any time" as inducements to prayer. In this regard, the seasonal sentence is much more applicable today than in the past, when the sentence was primarily connected not with the season or occasion, but with the act of confession to follow.

I have found it best when praying with a group several times per week to use the versicle most of the time, and to insert the seasonal sentence about once every week. This suits the sentence's function as a reminder of the sacred time, and also provides the element of flexibility. In private reading, I find that the sentence matters less. Sometimes I use the sentence, sometimes simply the classic versicle.

The *confession* was a late medieval innovation in monasteries and became widespread Anglican practice. Acts of confession were in fact unknown to the early church. The individual or private confession, of which this is a form, developed in the early Middle Ages in Celtic countries and flourished in the later Middle Ages, a markedly penitential period. Opening with confession all the time or even a majority of the time can lend a heavy and guilt-ridden feel to the liturgy, which is why the current *Book of Common Prayer* makes it strictly optional. It is included, however, because it is an appropriate way to begin the Office during Lent and any other penitential time, especially Fridays and Wednesdays, the ancient days of ascetic observance in the Christian church. I have found it helpful to employ the confession in this way, using it only on Fridays most of the year to set that day aside and to encourage reflection on the work week. I then employ it almost every day during Lent, and omit it throughout the season of Easter.

Two features of the confession should be noted. First, only one form for the confession is provided in Rite Two, and it is one of the few examples of a recent composition. There is strong theological reasoning at work here. The new confession emphasizes the complexity of sin as a matter of "thought, word, and deed," an understanding in tune with the Sermon on the Mount. The confession mentions "things done and left undone," reminding us that sin is not merely a matter of prohibited acts, but also a matter of negligence. It emphasizes the basis of sin as deficiency of love, and parallels love of God with love of neighbor. Finally, the confession concludes with a positive request that the result be to "delight in [God's] will, and walk in [God's] ways," suggesting that the most important point of confession, more than any other consideration, is to amend life and to restore a eucharistic attitude. These elements were surely present in the older form, which dates from the Reformation, but were less evident.

Second, there is an important rubric immediately after the absolution: "A deacon or lay person using the preceding form remains kneeling." The pronouncement of absolution of sins is one of the few prerogatives restricted to the Orders of bishop and priest, which is signified by their permission to stand. The rubric simultaneously guarantees, however, that the confession, like everything else in this service of worship, can be conducted in the absence of a priest—a guarantee of the nonclerical and corporate nature of the Office.

Invitatory Psalm

And now the first movement proper begins with an example of a genuine worship tradition: the use of the invitatory psalm. In the sixth century, Benedict of Nursia, whose *Rule* had enormous impact on the Western church, stipulated that Psalm 95 be the invitatory psalm every day. Since Benedict may have originated very little in his Rule, but rather organized and simplified current practice, the morning use of this psalm may be a great deal older than the sixth century. It might well predate the Office itself. Thus when we say Psalm 95, often called by its first word in Latin, *Venite* ("Come, let us…"), we are participating in a truly ancient tradition.

This psalm (or psalm fragment) "invites" us into the classic Judeo-Christian attitude of worship, which is joyful, vigorous praise: "Let us sing to the Lord; let us shout for joy to the rock of our salvation." Note that the two regular psalms appointed for this purpose, Psalms 95 and 100, are both addressed to fellow worshipers, not to God. Grammatically speaking they are not prayers at all, but prefaces to prayer. The word *invitatory* can mean more than invitation. The Latin word from which it derives can mean "entice" or "charm." This psalm is meant to charm us into worship. Prayer is many things, but above all, or beneath all, it is meant to be joyful and exhilarating, not tedious, strenuous, or painful.

Psalm 95, the *Venite*, is ideal for this purpose in alluding to God's tangible acts of creation, calling to mind the heights of the hills, the caverns of the earth, the sea, the dry land—all held in God's hand. These natural landscapes are stirring, and we respond to them with the joyous awe that is the raw material of worship. The imagery is deliberately beautiful and evokes Roman Catholic theologian Hans Urs von Balthasar's emphasis on the aesthetic aspect of theology: God as an artist. God creates things of beauty, and God creates us with the eyes, intelligence, feelings, and will required to appreciate these things. We are the audience for God's handiwork. We find ourselves deeply comforted and elated to realize that we are part of creation, for we, too, are "sheep of his hand." This discussion is not meant to be vaguely homiletic or inspiring, but is meant to illustrate the emotional usefulness of this psalm. It works by putting us in the very best mood for worship.

Another feature of this invitatory psalm is key. It is, in structure, a paradigmatic psalm. It works the way psalms work and exhibits the musical devices that make psalms what they are. First, it is simply but strongly metaphorical in the way it deliberately confuses animate and inanimate, divine and human. The Greek philosopher Xenophanes ridiculed religious people for their anthropomorphism, for making gods in human image, saying that if horses had hands they would make horselike gods. But the psalmist, more poet than philosopher, boldly anthropomorphizes in this short psalm fragment. We sing of a God with hands that hold caverns and mold dry land, like the hands of a cosmic giant. Yet at the same time, this God is a "rock"—that is, less than human.[8] We, on the other hand, are God's people and relate to God the way people relate to a king. Yet we are also "sheep" of God's pasture, vulnerable, dependent, and willful animals. All such characterization is more than literary decoration. It is central to what the psalm means, to what it says about God and about us.

Second, the psalm is typical in its parallelism. As biblical and literary scholars explain, the psalm form is based on parallel structures. In the first verse, we sing and then shout. The Lord Yahweh[9] is described as a "great God" and "a great King above all gods" (v. 3). These expressions all say the same thing, but say the same thing "in other words." The repetition adds subtle difference each time and allows a three-dimensional vision to emerge.

Third, and related to but not restricted to parallelism, is the mnemonic character of this psalm. It is easy to memorize. Anyone who prays this psalm as the invitatory will find that s/he has learned it by heart in a short period, even without intending to do so. This is because the parallelism, imagery, personification, and rhythms all impress the words into our consciousness. This psalm is typical of the Psalms and, to a lesser extent, of the entire Office in this aspect. Anyone who prays it daily will discover that s/he, without trying, is gradually learning the regular parts by heart.

The fragment of Psalm 95 offered in this part of the Office is the normal reading. But to allow for flexibility in practice there are two other possibilities throughout most of the year, and a deliberate departure for one season. First, a rubric encourages occasional use of the psalm in its entirety. Considerations of economy have dictated use of the shortened version on most days, but the fuller version allows a full and hearty praise song to start the day. Second, another classic psalm, the *Jubilate*, is offered as an alternative. Psalm 100, a short psalm offered in its entirety, accomplishes the same purpose as Psalm 95 but with slightly different imagery and a more universal sense of time and space. In fact, one can view the *Venite* and *Jubilate* as individual and collective versions of the basic impulse to praise. Psalm 95 addresses the individual, Psalm 100 "all you lands."

Normally, these two invitatory songs can be alternated daily, or one can be practiced for a stretch of time. Psalm 100 might be used twice a week for variety. Every group and individual will find a comfortable blend. In time, both can become habitual ways of opening both the Office and the day, and can be learned by heart, meaning not that they can be parroted word for word but that their dynamic and attitude can begin to inform the worshiper.

Since the earliest days of the Christian church, however, the fifty-day season of Easter has been set aside as distinctive. Acts of penance, penitence, or confession, ascetic practices, and mourning were not permitted. The entire season—one-seventh of the year—was understood as the Great Lord's Day, the "month of Sundays" wherein the eucharistic mood of joy and triumph was unbroken except for pastoral necessity. Our church has returned to this ancient practice in all sorts of ways, and in the Office we find a simple example. During Easter Week and, if desired, throughout the season (as the rubric in the middle of *BCP* 83 suggests), the invitatory psalm is replaced by a New Testament hymn, the *Pascha nostrum*. Familiar to most worshipers from its frequent use as the "Fraction Anthem" at the Eucharist, this amalgam of passages from the letters of Paul, beginning and ending and interspersed with the ancient shout of *Alleluia*, beautifully and powerfully reiterates the great themes of the paschal season: triumph, resurrection, life, sacrifice, feast, and festival. It also provides a strong element of seasonal variety.

To accompany the invitatory psalms and the *Pascha nostrum*, seasonal antiphons—short, lyrical scriptural sentences in two-part form—are offered (*BCP* 80–82). These serve the same function as the seasonal sentences above. They "tell us the time" theologically and locate the *kairos*. They also provide a frame for the invitatory that most find pleasing, and open musical possibilities for groups fortunate enough to explore musical settings. The name *antiphon* means "counterpointing" or "opposing" voices, and these are clearly designed in verse-response form for corporate prayer; therefore, most solitary practitioners omit them. Anyone praying alone might want to use just the first half of the sentence, if s/he finds the antiphon helpful.

The Psalm or Psalms

"Then follows the Psalm(s) appointed"—so the rubric now directs. The lectionary, found on pages 934–1001, does the "appointing," or the Psalter itself, if the officiant or individual chooses the daily psalm pattern dating to the first English prayer book. Unlike the invitatory, this normally is a full-length psalm or several short psalms read in sequence; occasionally, as in the case of Psalm 119, it is a substantial segment of a single psalm.

Most of us probably do not take the Psalms with enough seriousness. When was the last time you heard a sermon preached on a psalm? Or, if you are regularly called on to preach, when did you last preach on a psalm—or even mention a psalm in a sermon? We tend to think of psalms as a poetic or musical embellishment, as an interlude between the substantial lessons of Scripture. But in Scripture itself, and in the greater Christian tradition, psalms have always enjoyed preeminence. They were in essence a prayer book, and Jesus used them as such. Note how often Jesus quotes from the Psalms compared to other books of Scripture. The early church used the Psalms as the heart of their daily prayer. When the Benedictines and other monastics did the same, they were simply following an already ancient tradition.

So are we, when we give psalms that same pride of place in the Daily Office. It can even be said that the Office gives the Psalms a prominence found in no other prayer-book service. Although Psalms are used in every service and throughout the book, only in the Office are they prayed so consistently and sequentially. In the Eucharist, by contrast, they are read between other readings, providing a commentary and exercising a hingelike function. The ancient Office tradition, in monastery and cathedral practice alike, was always to read the entire Psalter in sequence. The current *Book of Common Prayer* alters this tradition only insofar as it gears the psalm sequence slightly more to the textures of the church year. Hence, in Lent there is more emphasis on the penitentials, in Easter more on the praise psalms. During any given year, anyone who prays the Office daily will still run through the Psalter as a whole nine or ten times, approximating the classic monthly sequence.

The Psalter in fact was the ancient "Book of Common Prayer," the prayer book of kings and prophets, of Jesus and the disciples. Countless Christians since have found it spiritually practical. Why should this be so? First and foremost, psalms are poetry, as already noted in the case of the invitatory. We may read them as if they were prose, but they are formally verse. In their original language they obey poetic conventions; they originally were sung, not said. This means that they are mnemonic, easily memorized. Even when not learned by heart, psalms tend to stay in the memory far better than prose. Presented in the prayer book in versified form, they can easily be reset to music when possible, and when not possible they are to be read as poetry.

Poetry is highly compact language. In Ezra Pound's definition, it is language "charged" to the fullest degree. Thus the Psalms express more than straightforward prose ever could. To appreciate this fact, consider what we have already observed about Psalm 95. A prose paraphrase might read, "Appreciate the sovereignty of God. God created various aspects of the physical reality we see, such as bodies of water, hills, caves, and even dry land. God also continues to protect these things." This paraphrase means almost exactly the same thing as

> In his hand are the caverns of the earth,
>   and the heights of the hills are his also.
> The sea is his, for he made it,
>   and his hands have molded the dry land. (vv. 4–5)

Yet, in a larger sense, the psalm means more than the paraphrase. Even in these two short lines, the poetic devices of personification, parallelism, alliteration, and rhythm "charge" the words, as Pound said. Even if we do not analyze such elements—and most of the time we do not—they are there, and they "work" on us. We feel the dynamic, personal aspects of God's creation, protection, and artistry in ways the paraphrase did not and could not touch.

I have just devoted more than one hundred words to two simple lines and have only scratched the surface of what they mean and do. This is the poetic reality of the Psalms, and not in an elite literary sense. Anyone with an open heart and mind senses these realities as s/he prays the Psalms.

Second, psalms are extraordinary in their range of theological feeling and expression. They cover the breadth and depth of human attitudes toward God in a way unmatched by any theological treatise. Try to think of an attitude or thought about God that does not appear in the Psalms. You may find this impossible. Have you doubted God's existence? Wondered how a good God can allow evil? Felt angry with God? Wished God would go away? would hurry up and act? would shower you with special favors? would take away some huge or tiny pain? The Psalms expressed these thoughts and feelings three millennia before you were conceived.

Consider Psalm 140, appointed for Friday morning in the first week of October—the Friday morning described in the preface. It is one of the psalms that have at times proved embarrassing to Christians. It is full of complaint, points the finger at other people, and is even, some would say, vaguely paranoid. "Protect me from the violent," the psalm says, "who are determined to trip me up." Medieval Christian commentators often allegorized such psalms. They dismissed the literal meaning as unimportant and pointed instead to an allegorical level at which the violent adversaries stood for demons, for spiritual enemies and not human opponents.

This may strike us as explaining the psalm away, but it seemed to work for centuries. Many Christians, in fact, accepted this method as the primary way to read psalms. What happens, however, when we take the psalm literally? What happened to those of us who read it that Friday in October? What happens whenever we read one of the challenging psalms?

Perhaps not much that we notice. At times we may be distracted, fatigued, or upset, and scarcely notice the psalm at all. But the regular practitioner of the Office soon learns to pay better attention and, surprisingly often, the Psalms live in all their clarity. Let us assume, then, that we are awake and aware on the day this psalm comes around again. What will we experience?

The initial line rings true: "Lord, deliver me from evildoers; / protect me from the violent." We may not feel this emotion immediately, but we have known it. Everyone knows what it is to fear those who do evil and to fear violence. Whether through childhood memories or adult anxieties, we all know the ghastly feeling of being afraid for one's physical being—and what a blessed relief it is to be delivered from such anxiety. The second line may at first seem more strained: "...who devise evil in their hearts / and stir up strife all day long." We may not feel quite so paranoid. Yet we have known that feeling as well. Even the well-adjusted person has known the feeling of persecution, of deliberate destruction aimed his or her way. Such is part of human life.

We have known the violent wishes, the fantasies of revenge, that ill-treatment inspires. Our nobler nature and our Christian identity may not be proud of such feelings and may want to deny them, but the psalm will not let that happen. It begs, "Let the evil of their lips overwhelm them. / Let hot burning coals fall upon them; / Let them be cast into the mire, never to rise again" (vv. 9–10). Although we shudder at this spitefulness, if we are honest we must admit that we have known such wishes.

In other words, such psalms force us to face the full range of our humanity and to bring it all before God—not just the lofty emotions and noble thoughts, but the angry, lustful, and weary thoughts. Praying the Psalms daily, or twice daily, through their full range, uncensored and evenly distributed, trains us to be honest with God in a most literal, most healthy way.[10]

Positive thoughts and feelings are equally well represented: gratitude, friendship, relief, erotic feelings, intellectual satisfaction. The full range of human responses, well documented by mystics and theologians, is expressed in the Psalms. The Psalms are eminently comprehensive and eminently human.

But no matter what the Psalms express, it is in the context of praise—the dominant theme of this first section of the Office. Some psalms mitigate or soften this theme; others accentuate and amplify it. It is, in fact, a distinctively Judeo-Christian teaching that, even in the midst of complaining or expressing pain or doubt, we can still praise God. Only if we thought nobody was listening would the praise and thanksgiving be silent.

As a guarantee, this first movement of the Office always ends with the *Gloria Patri*. This familiar short song of praise was first used, as far as we can discern, in this way. Forms of the Daily Office dating to the fourth century use the *Gloria Patri* as punctuation for the Psalms. Its origin is unclear. It does not appear in Scripture, although Paul uses similar forms in closing his letters, but its function in affirming the theme of praise is obvious.

The Lessons

The heart of the second "movement" of the Office, and its primary task, is the reading of Scripture; hence its title, "The Lessons." To many persons, especially those raised in a "free church" environment, but also perhaps to a number of Anglicans, Roman Catholics, and more traditional Protestants, this seems strange. "Bible study" is supposed to be apart from worship. Worship seems to use bits of Scripture as embellishment and as sermon material. The primary encounter between believer and Bible takes place outside worship—and outside "church"—in church school, perhaps, or in a classroom.

In fact, this attitude is a reversal of the way Scripture came into being and of its purpose for and relationship to the worshiping community. The most fundamental books—the Torah or Pentateuch, the first five books of the Old Testament, and the Gospels in the New Testament—were written to be read during weekly or daily worship and to be heard and interpreted in a large group. Other books were meant for other public gatherings. Certain psalms, for example, were written for coronations or weddings, and certain prophesies for penitential days. The Letters in the New Testament, with the exception of the few personal letters, were intended to be read aloud to entire congregations. Virtually no book in Scripture was intended to be studied on one's own or referred to at one's convenience. The private reading of the Bible and the small-group Bible study that seem so normal now would have seemed strange and dangerous to the Hebrews who produced the Old Testament and to the first generation of Christians who wrote the New Testament. These were public books, the common property of the Christian family, written to be read, proclaimed, and discussed in public.

All of which is simply to say that the public, daily reading of Scripture called for by the Daily Office is a return to the way Scripture was used and intended to be used. The church preceded the Bible—which is why it is so difficult to determine from the Bible alone what shape the church should take. There was no need for such a blueprint, since the church already existed. The Bible was not a worship manual, not a design for the church nor a prospectus—though many have tried to use the Bible in these ways. The Bible, rather, was always meant to remind humankind of the ways of God, to record God's acts in the past and humanity's response. It was meant as a covenant book, a book about an ongoing relationship strengthened by the daily reminder.

Thus, as suggested, the daily reading of Scripture in the Office amounts to an act of *anamnesis*, of ceasing to forget the historical revelation. Just as in the Eucharistic Prayer we remember the historical act of Jesus that instituted the rite ("On the night he was betrayed…"), each day we rehearse God's revelation. Often it will be a historical commemoration, a classic teaching, a prophecy. In any case, we claim that we hear God's Word. Within this second part of the Daily Office we listen to God. We are thus formed, informed, reformed, instructed, and reminded, comforted and challenged. Centuries of trial and error lie behind the current daily lectionary. It is thus the product of an enormously wide-ranging Christian experience. What then, exactly, is its plan?

Simply put, the Office lectionary provides for a sequential reading of Scripture over a two-year cycle, during which the Old Testament is read in nearly its entirety once, the New Testament twice, and the Psalms roughly fourteen times. In keeping with the rule of simplicity we have noted as a hallmark of the Office, the readings are always relatively brief. During the season after Pentecost, the readings are in course and general. During the seasons from Advent through Easter, they are geared to the seasonal themes, theology, and historical commemorations. For example, the Prophets are always emphasized in the Old Testament readings throughout Advent, postresurrection appearances of Jesus and the Book of Acts during the Great Fifty Days of Easter. During the Advent and Easter half of the liturgical year, the lessons are coordinated—Gospel, Old Testament, and New Testament readings often shedding light upon one another. The Psalms, similarly, are often seasonally appropriate, although they basically adhere to a seven-week course, replacing the monthly course originally devised by Thomas Cranmer. The monthly course, however, is also readily available, as the Psalter provides for days that each Psalm may be read.

This process may sound mechanical and schematic at first, but most who try the Office lectionary soon find it to be a compelling way of becoming involved with Scripture. It does not seem artificial, but natural and lively. Participants begin to look forward to the next day's reading. They begin to recall and to think about the readings throughout the day. If others in their group are also praying the Office, very often they begin to mention and to discuss the readings. Why?

Discussion happens because serial reading tends to be involving. For example, during the Christmas season, the twelve-day season that begins with the celebration of the Incarnation on December 24 or 25, the Daily Office readings provide a running commentary on the event. The Gospel readings present not only the nativity story, but also relevant background material. The Old Testament readings offer a minicourse in Old Testament typology, providing the sources and parallels behind so much Christian experience. Thus, while on the first Sunday after Christmas, at the Eucharist, we hear the splendid prologue to the Fourth Gospel, with its poetry about Word and Wisdom, in the weekday readings we hear the Old Testament context for that reading. On December 26, St. Stephen's Day, we hear the full story of his martyrdom in the selection from Acts for Morning Prayer. On the 28th, Holy Innocents, we hear the prophetic background to the commemoration of the children killed during Herod's search for the Christ child. Anyone who keeps up with the Office readings receives a depth and completion to the season available in no other way. The same obtains throughout the church year. The daily readings provide details, background, parallels—in short, the comprehensive scriptural context.

During the season after Pentecost, readings are in sequence for about six months. One year, for example, the Book of Deuteronomy is read practically in its entirety. In the next year, the Book of Numbers is read—books not often emphasized, let alone read through. The New Testament Epistles are read almost entirely, as are Acts and Revelation. The greater part of all four Gospels is reiterated or introduced. In short, the long season presents us with the opportunity for a patient, daily, sequential immersion in Scripture, and an ideal time for discerning larger themes, for extended study, for a new sense of our scriptural identity.

Recently the serial-reading dynamic was illustrated for me in a concrete way. A group within our parish reads Morning Prayer together on Thursdays. One of the women in the group read the Old Testament lesson, which came from the apocryphal book of Judith. She read the climax of the story, wherein the heroine, Judith, seduces the Assyrian general Holofernes into a drunken stupor. The story makes it clear that something terrible is about to happen to him and breaks off abruptly, in the manner of old-time radio serials that invited listeners to tune in the next day. And that was the effect on our reader: she told us, immediately after we were finished with the Office, "I've got to go read what happens next."

Our approach throughout has been practical. Now, what are the practical advantages, and the drawbacks, of this reading plan? One disadvantage is that it might be thought to stifle individual spontaneity and inspiration. The Bible, except in an abstract theological sense, is not a single book but a collection of books—a library—and most people like to browse and explore libraries from time to time. Another disadvantage is that the daily quantity of Scripture may seem too short and limited, like being restricted to reading a good book at the rate of two pages a day. Finally, even though the lectionary is, as I have noted, intentional and rationally arranged, parts may seem arbitrary and even irrelevant to what may be going on in the individual's personal, parish, or professional life.

Most faithful followers of the lectionary will experience all these drawbacks. The lectionary is neither ideal nor perfect. But most will also quickly appreciate the advantages as far outweighing these drawbacks. First, it truly is a common lectionary in that countless others are reading the same portions of Scripture on any given day. This is a source of yet untapped and unrealized strength. For example, if one knows that several others in a parish are reading the same spiritual materials every day, the sense of community inherent in that fact can be significant. How much greater the realization that across the church tens of thousands are reading the same lections?

The second strength in this system of reading is its incremental nature. It is, in fact, an example of the educational trend of spiral learning. Every two years the cycle begins anew. Anyone who goes through the cycle more than once begins to remember the readings from the previous cycle, and to remember his or her thoughts and associations. Each successive reading reveals previously unnoticed aspects. As the literary critic Eric Auerbach suggests, Scripture tends to be all depth, with very little surface, such that even daily readings begin to seem inexhaustible, like a deep well, in their richness and textures.

To experience this depth and breadth does take intentionality. Certain ways of reading Scripture seem to work better than simply skimming, which is the way we approach business letters or newspapers. Through the centuries, various systems have been devised for appropriating Scripture. For our purposes, a few gentle hints should suffice. Probably the gravest danger in Office reading is the same as at Sunday's Eucharist—that, unless we are intentional, the readings will "wash over" us, leaving us unchanged. This happens even when we ourselves are reading. Unless we have a reason to retain what we read, we treat reading passively and fail to deposit the content into even our short-term memories. Think for example of the lighter portions of yesterday's newspaper. How much do you remember? A method of meditation based on the teachings of François de Sales that many have found helpful is to determine at each session to retain some element of the reading. This could be a phrase, an image, a piece of narrative plot, a problematic question, or even a single word. De Sales compared the process to picking a small bunch of flowers any time you visited a public garden. Deciding to retain something, however small, almost guarantees that it will happen. When we begin that practice, it has the cumulative effect of guiding us into a relevant reading of Scripture.

If one is praying the Office alone, of course, one simply reads the lesson in silence. Even in this case, the ancient practice of slow reading with the lips moving, or whispering, works for many as a more meditative mode. Solitary reading offers several advantages. The reading can be interrupted, notes made, and words and phrases underlined since no listener is expecting a smooth and uninterrupted reading.

This discussion raises the issue of the art of hearing Scripture. Most modern people are more facile at private reading, which is, after all, a major way we ingest information. And although most are accustomed to audio-visual media as well, they are not versed in listening. There is a profound difference between watching television, or listening to the radio, and being read to. It requires practice for most people, but is well worth the time. Most discover that, once they practice the art of listening to Scripture, they begin to notice and retain things they never noticed when reading in solitude.

Here again the Salesian principle works. When we listen to a passage with the intention of retaining even a single word or phrase, we are much more likely to accomplish that objective. In time, the practice becomes automatic. If praying the Office with others, another possibility is to follow along in a translation different from the one being read aloud. This simple technique provides a "binocular" experience of Scripture that illuminates obscure passages and sheds new light on familiar readings. Those who are able have found similar value in following along in another language, such as Luther's German translation or the Douay-Rheims French version. Reading in the Latin Vulgate provides a window into the version of Scripture that the Western church used for centuries before anyone read the Bible in a modern language. Those who have studied either of the original biblical languages can enjoy a closeness to the Word, and can keep their language skills honed, by reading along in the Hebrew or Greek. Anyone praying the Office alone is also free to try these methods, but only those who pray in a group get the binocular effect.

Whatever the setting, anyone who prays the Office for an extended period will find that the readings raise questions, from simple questions of detail to large theological and ethical issues. This is part of the intention of the lectionary, part of the use of Scripture itself. A simple response many find useful is to read with the help of a commentary. One may consult a commentary before or after the Office, or, if reading alone, immediately after a reading.

Interesting as such apparatus may be, the fundamental purpose of the lessons is not intellectual stimulation but spiritual formation. Therefore, most of the time the classic approaches to spiritual reading will prove most useful. We have already briefly outlined the *Salesian* approach. The *Ignatian* approach is defined in exhaustive detail in Ignatius Loyola's *Spiritual Exercises*, a manual for an intensive, month-long formation. Ignatius's approach to Scripture is simple and easily adaptable to the brief lessons in the Office. He aimed for total involvement of the person in Scripture, a contemporary-sounding goal. To this end, he believed that imagination, reason, emotions, and the will could all be involved in hearing or reading the Bible. A modified and abbreviated Ignatian technique would be to spend a few moments after each reading (1) reasoning through a given passage; (2) relating to the passage emotionally; and (3) making a simple resolution to carry out some small action based on the reading. When the reading seems suitable, an exercise might involve picturing the scene or story and imagining the textures, sounds, and odors, thus locating ourselves in the passage. Not all texts invite this response, but many do: Old Testament narratives, Gospel parables, incidents in the Book of Acts, and so on. In any event, this modified Ignatian exercise should take only a few moments. Anything lengthier will distort the rhythm of the Office.

The third classic meditative approach is older still. It is the simple technique practiced by the *Benedictines* from their inception in the sixth century and by the desert forebears. This approach involves repeating a portion of the reading, perhaps a phrase or word, until it becomes part of one's consciousness. Medieval monastic commentators compared this to the ruminative process of a beast "chewing the cud." This homely image captures the technique's down-to-earth feel. The technique precludes intellectualizing and guarantees that the content of the second movement of the Office is retained throughout the day.

Any of these methods, or none, can be practiced in the silence the rubric encourages after the readings (*BCP* 84). For the first time, such silence is "officially" permitted, but long before the current edition of the *Book of Common Prayer* many groups and individuals found the silence desirable and observed it. We have compared the Office in shape to musical forms, among other things. The analogy is especially apt here. Like silences in music, the silences after the readings and at other points are not a cessation of activity, but part of the mode and meaning. Any of the methods for hearing Scripture described above can be practiced in the silences after the readings. Conversely, nothing need happen—nothing deliberate and purposeful, at any rate. The person praying the Office can keep silence as a moment of receptivity, of waiting or rest. Often, in fact, this will prove the most helpful use for the silences.

You may find that you need to practice keeping the silence. The person praying the Office in solitude may be tempted to save time and to omit it. Groups may find the silence even more easily omitted. Within a group everyone is conscious of one another's time constraints, and, above all, years of conditioning to the expectations of courtesy make us feel that silences are to be avoided. We speak of an "awkward" silence, a "pregnant" pause. Indeed, convincing people to keep silence together may be even more difficult than convincing them to pray together.

The experience of many, however, is that the silence, once practiced, becomes a necessary part of praying the Office. At the simplest level, the person praying alone finds that the silence helps immeasurably with assimilating the Word and with the concentration necessary for prayer. Groups praying together find the same holds true and that, unexpectedly, keeping silence in a group proves more valuable than in solitude. The group seems to "find" its own sense of silence, and the individuals reinforce each other's concentration.

The duration of the silence is not specified. For it to have much value at all, however, it should probably be substantial. Some have found a one minute to work well; it is surprising how long a minute's silence can seem to a group first starting and unaccustomed to public silence. Another possibility is to let the silence match the time it takes to read the text aloud. In "larger" contexts—the Office said in a cathedral or seminary, for example, where the agreed time expenditure is already unusually substantial—the silence might be prolonged for several minutes. Such a period seems strange to the newcomer but positively delicious, a luxury, to the veteran of the Office.

In the latter situation, many practice centering prayer or Zen technique during the silence, practices that demand several minutes, at least. Those who find themselves drawn to such spiritual practice can easily join it to the Daily Office by scheduling their longer period of silence immediately beforehand, allowing ten minutes, say, of centering prayer before the officiant begins. This works well for many in the parish setting, where the Office must end "on time" in order for everyone to get on with business. Arriving ten minutes early allows one to fuse a refreshing experience of silence with the strengthening experience of the Office. The individual praying in solitude is free to use silence, for any duration, at any point.

Even a few seconds of silence, however, kept after one or two readings, can provide a meaningful, welcome element in the Daily Office. Our world is suffused with noise, and we are saturated with words. An island of silence in the midst of hearing the Word can do wonders to plant that Word within us. Like so many features of the Office, silence can become a gift.

The Canticles

The canticles invariably follow the readings. The word *canticulum* means "song" (or "little song") in Latin; *psalmos* means "song" in Greek. What is the difference, then, between a canticle and a psalm? None, in form. All psalms and canticles are written in biblical song format, reflected in the way they are laid out in the *Book of Common Prayer*. There is also no difference in origin. All are translations of songs from Hebrew or Greek. The difference is that we conventionally call "psalms" only those songs collected in the book that bears that name. All other biblical songs, in any other book, are styled "canticles." Some of these canticles are as old as— some older than—the Psalms themselves. The New Testament canticles and the two canticles written later than the Bible are centuries later in date.

There is, moreover, no difference in function between canticles and psalms. The canticles as a genre are praise songs, and the canticles provided in the prayer book for use with the readings all fall into this category. Thus they recapitulate the eucharistic theme of the first portion of the Office. Any morning canticle may be considered appropriate for any day. That statement should probably be emphasized. Canticles may be chosen at random, or by personal preference. Anyone who grows attached to the Song of Moses (Canticle 8), let us say, is free to use that canticle every day for a month following the Old Testament lesson. I have done that sort of thing myself, for the joy of truly getting to know a canticle.

At the same time, the facility of the Office in sanctifying chronological time extends to the days of the week, and an intelligent weekly canticle sequence is the first clear instance of this facility. Certain canticles are especially appropriate for certain days, so a distribution of canticles is suggested (*BCP* 144), with canticles chosen for their association with certain days. The Te Deum is used for the Lord's Day, for example, and the Song of Moses, with its Passover-night connotations, for Thursdays. An important word choice here is *suggested*, as opposed to the usual prayer-book word *appointed*. These canticles are especially appropriate for given days, but flexibility is also appropriate. For example, on a day when thanksgiving seems in order, the Sunday canticles make sense; at a time when sin or suffering is evident, Canticles 14 and 19 may be helpful.

But let us examine the canticles one by one in the order suggested for the week. For Sundays, the canticle after the Old Testament lesson is the *Benedictus* or Song of Zechariah, the praise uttered by father of John the Baptist (Luke 1:68–79).[11] It is a dynamic canticle, full of powerful verbs, and bridges the Old and New Testaments. It has a "triumphal Christology"—that is, it depicts the work of Christ as a victory over death and sin and darkness, rather than as a painful sacrifice. It ends on a lovely and quiet note: "...the dawn from on high shall break upon us, / To shine on those who dwell in darkness and the shadow of death, and to guide our feet into the way of peace." This was the only canticle used at this point in the monastic Office, since it perfectly suited the purpose of a morning canticle between Old and New Testament readings. (Alternates to this canticle for Sundays in certain seasons are suggested below.)

The second canticle for Sundays was the regular second canticle in Matins—another term for Morning Prayer—the *Te Deum*. According to legend, Ambrose and Augustine composed this in tandem, alternating lines spontaneously. Since Ambrose is associated strongly with sermons and music, Augustine with theology and vision, this pairing is symbolically valid. Modern scholars have suggested that this prayer-poem may be a fragment of a eucharistic prayer of the earliest church. If so, it is even more appropriate as the climactic canticle at Morning Prayer: a song of praise and thanksgiving in three parts, that is, trinitarian in structure, beginning with the simplest statement of fact and truth—"You are God: we praise you." This canticle, based on Isaiah and Revelation, is full of the imagery of the Kingdom of God, rehearses the Incarnation and the victory over death—demonstrating, like the *Benedictus*, a triumphal theology—and ends with eschatological hope: "Bring us with all your saints / to glory everlasting."

Canticle 9, *Ecce, Deus*, the First Song of Isaiah, is suggested for Mondays. The monastic breviary used it for one of the minor Morning Offices. According to Old Testament scholarship, the poem celebrates the Israelite return from exile, but it works perfectly as a morning canticle at the beginning of the work week, since it also looks forward. The canticle states that the Lord "will" do good things for you; you "shall" do this and that in thankful response. It works in other words as a preparatory praise song, and as a bracing, challenging poem to repeat on a Monday morning. Canticle 19, *Magna et mirabilia*, the Song of the Redeemed, is suggested as the second canticle, and is also suggested for Saturdays and Thursdays in Lent. It is in the mode of Isaiah 6, expressing awe at God's majesty. God is "ruler of the universe" and "king of all the ages," giving us a transcendent perspective that is helpful at stressful times, such as the beginning of the work week or during Lent. The message of the prayer is that God surpasses human understanding in God's greatness, and that all nations will eventually fall down and worship God. The poem suggests eternity and the eschatological perspective that Christians have always found comforting.

Canticle 13, *Benedictus es, Domine*, the Song of the Three Young Men, is suggested for Tuesday morning. It is unique among the canticles in its form as an extended *Gloria*. Those who use it frequently will notice its neat weaving and variations in thought and image. Its content—praising God for cosmic creation—reinforces the idea of the days of the week replicating the days of creation. The second canticle suggested for Tuesday, the *Dignus es* (Canticle 18), continues the praise motif but addresses praise in part to Christ, making it a perfect companion to Canticle 13. We will examine it more closely below, since it is also suggested for Friday.

In the contemporary Western world, Wednesday is the midweek day. In classic Christianity it is the first, and lesser, of the "station" days, which since the earliest church have been weekdays of special observance, appropriate for weekly practices of self-denial such as fasting and vigils.[12] Thus the first canticle, Canticle 11, the *Surge, illuminare,* is a canticle of expectation, a classic "station" or vigil canticle. It is also, therefore, suggested for other days during Advent and Lent, which look forward to other things. Praying and singing it regularly reminds us that, at several levels, we Christians are waiting for a consummation that none of us has seen but that we should regularly imagine. The second canticle is Canticle 16, the Song of Zechariah, that we have already examined. Again, repetition of the canticles, staggered through the week, creates a "weaving" effect that subtly associates the days and reiterates important theological themes.

Thursdays are naturally associated with Holy (or "Maundy") Thursday, the day of Christ's Last Supper and betrayal, the agony in the Garden of Gethsemane, the institution of the Lord's Supper, and the beginning of the climax of the passion. As such, the first canticle is Canticle 8, the *Cantemus Domino,* the song of victory Moses offers after the deliverance from Egypt and crossing the sea, reflecting the Passover history. From the earliest days, Christians have understood Passover as a foreshadowing or first run of the passion itself—the Christian story in a different key, as it were. The second canticle suggested is the "major" *Gloria, Gloria in excelsis* (Canticle 20), with its strong eucharistic connotations that reinforce the theme of a Thursday eucharistic supper. Like the *Te Deum,* it is magnificent (and extrabiblical), serving to link the day with the Lord's Day to come.

Friday is above all the day of the crucifixion, a connotation that has made the day significant to many Christians who honor no other weekday. The first canticle suggested is *Quaerite Dominum,* the

Second Song of Isaiah (Canticle 10), the only regularly suggested canticle that emphasizes repentance and, to a degree, the absence rather than the presence of God. It also emphasizes the creation theme that appears throughout the week. Friday is the day when animals, including humankind, were created, and so the emphasis is on "seed for sowing and bread for eating," the notion of human activity as the climax of creation, and on God's "word," which "will accomplish that which [God] has purposed," a line that gains poignancy in the light of the day's associations with Good Friday.

Saturday is, despite confusion in some Christian circles, the Sabbath day, when God rests and beholds creation in its goodness and perfection. Canticle 12, a Song of Creation, does exactly that. A praise poem, like most canticles, it categorizes creation into the cosmic order, the earth and its creatures, and humankind, and encourages their praise of God. The second canticle, *Magna et mirabilia* (Canticle 19), stresses God's transcendence. Theologically, it is an *apophatic* as opposed to a *kataphatic* song, emphasizing that God "surpasses human understanding." The canticle makes a neat balance to the kataphatic, positive assertions made the rest of the week and is also appointed for days during the penitential seasons.

Since the Judeo-Christian week begins on Sunday, Saturday completes the cycle. One canticle, however, is not regularly suggested, but is reserved for the penitential seasons—Canticle 14, the Song of Penitence, *Kyrie Pantokrator*. This vivid song is unique among the canticles because its theme of penitence rivals the theme of joyful praise. Its structure is curious. It begins on the same note of cosmic praise seen in several canticles—"You made the heavens and the earth, with all their vast array"—but then introduces a new idea by stating that "all things quake with fear at your presence; they tremble because of your power." This fear and trembling is new along with everything that follows: the prophetic "You hold back your hand; you do not punish as we deserve"; the prayerful equivalent of wishful thinking in the affirmation "you have promised forgiveness to sinners"; and the final half of the canticle, which begins, "And now, O Lord, I bend the knee of my heart." The last seven lines focus on the speaker. The word "I" appears repeatedly as in no other canticle. These lines are a full confession, and beg for God's characteristic mercy: "I have sinned,

O Lord, I have sinned, and I know my wickedness only too well." Nowhere else in the canticles is there such a focus on the ego or the singular speaker; nowhere else is heard this expression of pain and awareness of sin. If we follow the prayer book's suggestion, we will voice this confession only during Lent—but several times throughout the week, more often than any other canticle. The prayer lends a strong penitential flavor to that season. Yet even this song ends as it begins, with praise. For in Lent, that is the proper response to ultimate reality.

At this point, an essential dynamic of Morning Prayer should be clear. In examining four elements—invitatory psalm, psalm, readings, and canticles—one notices that two elements vary widely. The psalm, or combination or portion of psalms, will not be repeated, normally, for seven weeks. The lessons recur only once every two years. Two elements, by contrast, are consistent: the invitatory, which has little variation, and the canticles, which are repeated at least once a week. Within the psalms and lessons, of course, there is great variety. The Psalms range, as suggested, from sublime hymns of praise to "terrible" psalms that complain, curse, and shudder. The lessons within their two-year course cover virtually the entirety of Holy Scripture, and exhibit even greater range, including the rich mixture of human and divine that constitutes the Bible. Between psalms and readings, therefore, lies a staggering range of human thought and feeling. These texts force us to confront our anger, despair, vengefulness, lust, and greed, as well as our noblest aspirations and highest sense of fellowship with God.

The invitatory and the canticles, by contrast, express one theme with little variation, which is the eucharistic theme of thanksgiving and praise. They are always, even during penitential seasons, "positive"; they always find reasons for exultation and give us voice to express exultation. Sometimes these elements stand in creative contrast with the readings. Sometimes they reinforce one another. This dynamic is part of the power in the Daily Office.

Let us consider two examples of this tension. On a Sunday in August, during Year One in the readings, we slowly work through the heartrending story of the rebellion of Absalom, King David's haughty, handsome, and beloved son. It is a story rich with background irony and heavy with intrigue. Absalom had once arranged a violent death for his half-brother Amnon, who had violated Absalom's beautiful sister, and thus had repaid treachery for treachery. Like a Greek tragic hero, Absalom bore guilt for this act. Later, David's trusted counselor, the brilliant strategist Ahithophel, turned traitor and seduced Absalom into a revolt that nearly succeeded.

On a Wednesday morning ten days later we come to the pitiful ending, as David, having put down the revolt, hears of the death of Absalom. The danger is past and David's duty as king has been fulfilled, but there is no place for the joy of victory. David at last can express his feelings as a father and mourns Absalom with the cry that has echoed, "O my son Absalom, my son, my son Absalom! Would I had died instead of you, O Absalom, my son, my son!" (2 Sam. 18:33).

Throughout the story we have seen the shadow of treachery and violence from David's own entirely human history. Therefore, we cannot feel that the suffering is "unjust," but it is nevertheless painful if we have read with sympathy. David's fate and its inevitability touches our humanity. Yet we follow the story with a canticle. If we follow the daily cycle, the canticle is the Third Song of Isaiah, which in part reads: "Arise, shine, for your light has come, and the glory of the Lord has dawned upon you." That song, with its hopeful vision of Zion, balances the story that has just concluded. It quietly reminds us that, in the Christian vision, the story does not end until the city of Zion is realized.

On Friday, in the third week of either lectionary year, we repeat Psalm 88—one of the darkest of the "terrible" psalms. It is in a sense even more terrible than the imprecatory psalms, the "cursing" psalms that rain horrible fantasies on one's enemies. The dialogue of Psalm 88 is strictly between the speaker and God and expresses a brutal mix of despair and self-pity: "I am full of trouble; my life is at the brink of the grave. / I am counted among those who go down to the pit; / I have become like one who has no strength...." It is so bleak that medieval commentators saw the poem as forecasting Christ's feelings from the cross.

Nevertheless, if we are honest, we have to admit that we recognize the feelings of alienation, abandonment, futility, and despair. If we do not know the feelings personally, then we know them in a larger human sense. When we look back to the Holocaust, apartheid, Hiroshima and Nagasaki, and the two global wars, we can speak this psalm without hesitation; we can own it. It gives voice to the nihilism and despair that any human being feels from time to time.

Against Psalm 88 is balanced the invitatory, which, if we follow the suggestion in the Office, is Psalm 95. Read in its entirety, it includes not only the song of triumph we hear on many mornings but also the warning: "Harden not your hearts, as your forebears did in the wilderness, at Meribah, and on that day at Massah, when they tempted me." It thus becomes a bracing proclamation of God's sovereignty and power and beauty and goodness: a perfect counterweight to Psalm 88. I choose the word *counterweight* deliberately. The force of saying (or singing) these psalms in tandem is not contradiction or nonsense but the articulation of two theological truths, two realities, neither of which must be denied. The Christian faith affirms both the reality of despair and the sovereignty of God.

The primary theme of Morning Prayer is eucharistic in its thanksgiving and praise, and in its focus on what we owe God. However, this is not the whole of reality as we well know. Daily thanksgiving and praise, healthy as it is, does involve the spiritual risk of failing in solidarity with the most miserable. Psalm 88 unites us emotionally and spiritually with prisoners, refugees and exiles, and the diseased. Whenever we pray such a psalm we join our voice to theirs, and we remember them. It does not cancel our praise and thanksgiving but, on the contrary, makes it real.

The Prayers

Only now, having heard God's Word and having reminded ourselves briefly of our covenantal relationship with God, are we ready to express our concerns and to "ask God for what we want." I urge anyone actively praying the Office to try a simple experiment. Just before praying the Office, make a list of things to pray about. Then, a few minutes later, having heard the lessons and repeated the Creed, see if you do not find your list modified. This often will happen and is encouraged by the shape of the Office itself. Scripture informs our prayer life, and it does so in a most immediate and vivid way for those who pray the Office.

The prayers themselves begin with the paradigmatic scriptural prayer, the Lord's Prayer or Our Father. My guess is that, even if you know no other prayers by heart, you know this prayer, which is undoubtedly the best-known prayer in the Christian world.

There are good reasons for familiarity with the Our Father. It is the prayer "our Savior Christ has taught us," as we say during the Eucharist; that is, it has "dominical authority." Because Jesus taught it, Christians have almost always regarded it as the perfect prayer. That is why the Lord's Prayer is placed at the climactic point in the Eucharist.[13] But that is not where it appears now in the Office. Rather, it heads the section labeled simply "The Prayers"—the intentional intercessions, thanksgivings, and petitions that amount to our "input" in the Office. In other words, the Lord's Prayer opens the sections in which we address God. In the Eucharist, the Our Father is climactic; in the Office, it is paradigmatic.

The Lord's Prayer comes first to inform all the prayers that follow. To appreciate it fully and to understand its usefulness in the Office, we can try another experiment. In one of Plato's dialogues, the *Euthyphro*, a basic question arises. Are certain things moral because God commands them, or does God command certain things because they are moral? Either answer raises theological problems, but that is a subject for theology. We can ask a version of the same question: Is the Lord's Prayer great because Jesus said it, or did Jesus devise the prayer because it is great? The answer in this case is simple. It is great and would be as great even were someone else the author.

With its beginning in praise, its eschatology, its simple, physical, material petition, its central confession and bold association of God's forgiveness with our forgiveness of others, its dire allusion to the "time of trial" and climactic prayer for deliverance from evil, the Lord's Prayer is like poetry in its "charged" or dense quality. Few five-sentence arrangements in any language have accomplished so much. You probably memorized this prayer at an early age, yet you still use it. Presumably, unlike other teachings memorized as a child, you still find it useful. The Our Father is like a well. We return to it throughout life and draw water, yet never seem to exhaust it.

I have called the prayer *paradigmatic* because it teaches and sets the pattern for what follows. This is important because most people when praying spontaneously, no matter how well they have been taught, tend to offer petition after petition. They may "know better," yet for many people petition almost "is" prayer. Most unchurched people pray at crisis moments, when petition is their best recourse. Practicing Christians tend to revert to childhood patterns such as "saying one's prayers," which are largely the same thing.

The Our Father neatly counterbalances this tendency. Only one of its petitions is a petition in the sense of asking God for a favor. Although brief, the Lord's Prayer accomplishes a great deal. Because of its familiarity it may be difficult to see what it does express. When we grasp what it says, we then can grasp its significance in the context of the Office. Again, we need to appreciate and experience that "charged" quality. Perhaps no set of words has said so much in so little space.

The Lord's Prayer begins with relationship by stating that God is "Our Father in heaven." That God relates to us as a parent is the most important image of God in the New Testament. Surprisingly, the image is scarcely represented in the Old Testament, but it was the primary way Jesus understood his relationship to God. We are encouraged in the Lord's Prayer to call God "Father," *Abba*, as Jesus did, a word that approaches the meaning of the toddler's "papa." The mention of "heaven" affirms our trust and belief in another world, another dimension to reality.

The three phrases that follow are all doxology (praise), including the blessing of the name; the eschatological welcoming of the kingdom, which echoes the primary theme of Jesus' earthly teaching; and personal submission, expressing one's wish that God's will be done and that, thereby, earth become like heaven. This opening parallels the opening of the Office as we have understood it, as a grand movement centered in praise and establishing a relationship.

Next comes the single, simple petition asking God to give us this day our daily bread. It is impossible for the Christian to think of bread without biblical echoes of bread from the ground in Genesis and in Jesus' teaching and experience: Jesus as the bread of life, bread as substance broken and shared, and bread multiplied to feed multitudes. For us bread is both humble and familiar, and the most transcendent and miraculous of substances. It is God-given and God-revealing. None of this thought is abstruse but simply recounts the biblical "setting" for bread.

On the other hand, "bread" stands for other things. It is synecdoche for "supply us with our genuine wants and needs." We do not require theological instruction to understand this fact. Any child who learns this prayer realizes this intuitively. We as creatures are dependent every day. We require elements such as water and air, provided in the opening chapters of Genesis, almost continually. This is not a difficult thought but is easily forgotten—that is what we mean by "taking things for granted." Serious repetition of the Lord's Prayer reminds us not to take things for granted. The petition for bread sets the tone for subsequent prayers for needs small and vast, local and personal, immediate and long-range—physical, spiritual, intellectual, and emotional.

Prayers for mutual forgiveness follow and a proportionate promise established as we ask as much forgiveness from God as we are willing to give others. In other words, the prayer extends the relationship with God that we have just affirmed to include our relationship with others—a "horizontal" rather than a "vertical" extension. On occasion, we focus our need for forgiveness even more sharply through confession, but the daily affirmation of that need is always present in the Lord's Prayer.

The next petition, "save us from the time of trial"—which in the traditional version appears in the somewhat misleading euphemism, "lead us not into temptation"—again reflects a basic element in the vision of Jesus himself. Jesus envisioned that a time of trial, a cataclysmic era, was "about" to arrive and that we would need special protection. This is easily forgotten in the daily texture of human experience, which is by definition not cataclysmic. The Our Father serves as a daily reminder that our faith has an ultimate aim and takes the reality of apocalypse seriously.

This serious aspect continues in the next petition for deliverance from evil. This phrase is closely related to the baptismal covenant, wherein we renounce the forces of evil, Satan, and sinful desires. This struggle, too, is a daily reality, not an occasional occurrence. Every day we are drawn away from God and toward self and sin. The forces of evil may be most dangerous when we are least aware of this reality. The Lord's Prayer forewarns us of the danger, and pleads God's help in resisting evil.

The prayer ends as it begins, on the note of praise. Many scholars tell us that this was a conventional prayer ending in Jesus' time, but that the future thrust—"now and forever"—was a new element. The structure parallels, as we shall see, the closing rites of the Daily Office, making the Lord's Prayer a virtual microcosm of the Office itself. Or, better, the Office can be understood as an expansion of the Lord's Prayer.

The Lord's Prayer, like the Office as a whole, begins and ends with praise and places intercession, petition, and confession in between. Further, it addresses present, past, and future concerns, with a general thrust toward the future—an "eschatological" thrust. Again we can say that the Office is like music, in which a theme stated in a small space is often amplified into a larger composition.

The Suffrages

The second stage involves one of several sets of suffrages (from the Latin *suffragium*, "voting tablet"). The form is a dialogue, in which the officiant says one line and the participants respond. This process reinforces a corporate sense. Even when only two persons are praying, they have to work together and pay attention to one another. The Lord's Prayer works equally well as a solitary prayer—in some senses, it is better that way—but the suffrages are clearly meant for two or more, reminding us that when two or three are gathered God will stand among them. My own practice, therefore, is to omit the suffrages when praying alone—the only portion of the Office that seems to make no sense in those circumstances.

The suffrages are among the most traditional elements in the *Book of Common Prayer*. By "traditional," I mean more than "whatever I grew up with." The word *traditio* refers to the "handing down" of ideas, forms, and values from generation to generation. In this sense, the current *Book of Common Prayer* is the most traditional version of an English-language prayer book ever produced.[14] It contains more ancient, medieval, and early-modern material than any previous worship book.[15]

I refer specifically also to Anglican tradition. The *Book of Common Prayer* is an assembly of prayers from all centuries and all parts of the world, but three especially creative eras are most substantially represented: the era of the undivided church (roughly 100–600 C.E.); the early modern era (roughly the sixteenth and seventeenth centuries); and the twentieth century. The suffrages, as an easily recognizable version of the suffrages offered in the first *Book of Common Prayer* of 1549, are a distinctly early-modern phenomenon, adapted for modern and American concerns.

The suffrages are, in other words, one of Thomas Cranmer's contributions. They are not, however, his composition. Every verse and response derives from the Psalms—again reinforcing the unity of the Office, and giving scriptural warrant for this crucial portion of the Office's third movement. In a sense, the suffrages are simply a tissue of psalm phrases, continuing the strong psalm orientation we have seen throughout. All prayer-book tradition, from all periods in the history of the church, ultimately derives from Scripture interpreted, adapted, and pressed into service. Most important, because the suffrages are psalm verses in form, they share the aesthetic strengths we have already discerned generally in the Psalms. They are rhythmic, largely in parallel, imagistic and symbolic, and memorable.

The suffrages also relate the Office to the other sacraments, to the Eucharist in particular, since they voice the same prayer concerns. In the context of Eucharist, prayer is offered for (1) the universal church, (2) the nation and all in authority, (3) the welfare of the world, (4) the concerns of the local community, (5) those who suffer, and (6) the departed. These concerns are stated specifically on page 359 and are meant to guide the petitions offered at a eucharistic celebration. The Office suffrages initiate a process of prayer that encompasses these same concerns. Suffrages A prays for the church, nation, suffering people, and the world. The dead are movingly mentioned in the second set of suffrages for Evening Prayer. In the course of the collects, free intercessions, and prayer for mission that follow, the list is made complete as we articulate more specific concerns of the community.

The Collects

The collects, or collect, follow the suffrages. In contrast to the Eucharist, wherein the collect practically opens the service, in the

Office it follows the Lord's Prayer and the general suffrages. This is in keeping with the nature of the Office, which is less focused on specific occasions and more "repeatable." The function of the collect, however, remains the same: it expresses a theological theme, draws together as many elements of the rite as possible, commemorates, and specifies.

Yet the Office allows for, even seems to encourage, the use of more than one collect. How can this be explained? In a sense, multiple collects are redundant or contradictory. The ancient liturgies used a single collect to sum up themes of the day and to gather prayer intentions, which is why the Eucharist always uses one collect. But the Office, being more general in theme, can accommodate more than one. The Benedictines established an early custom of three collects, and our prayer-book Office is based loosely on that custom.

In praying the Office we would normally use the Collect of the Day (*BCP* 211–61), one of the collects for the day of the week (98–100), and one of the three prayers for mission (100–101). On the majority of weekdays there is no Collect of the Day. On these days we use the collect from the preceding Sunday, typically spelled out in the calendar that begins the prayer book.

Closing Prayers

The Daily Office may end at this point. All three major tasks have been achieved; the three movements—doxology, anamnesis, supplication—have been played. We have sung God's praises, listened to God's Word, and told God what we want. Everything from this point on is optional. In fact, as already noted, the hymn and free intercessions are also optional. Once the prayer for mission has been said, the Office may end.

However, we almost never end the Office in this way. We feel the need for "the sense of an ending," to borrow a phrase from literary critic Frank Kermode. The Office, of course, is not literature but a conversation, yet the same principle is relevant. In casual conversation, unless we are interrupted, we feel the need for conclusion. We say, "Well, I have to be going," or "Goodbye"—itself a blessing in origin, meaning "God be with you." We close letters with "sincerely," or a similar formula. We do not simply sign them. We feel the need, likewise, for closure in this conversation with God.

The *Book of Common Prayer* presents a series of options for closing. Previous editions specified all the following elements. The current *Book of Common Prayer*, ever flexible, allows us to choose. The first option is a classic Prayer of Thanksgiving dating from the seventeenth century and first included in the 1662 Book of Common Prayer, customarily referred to as the "General Thanksgiving." Composed, or compiled, by Bishop Reynolds of Norwich,[16] it remains a splendid, brief but comprehensive expression of the eucharistic attitude toward God. The thanksgiving thus recapitulates the themes of Part One, ending the Office on the same note with which it began and leaving us with "thankful hearts." It is among the most intelligent and meaningful of prayers from the formative Anglican era.

Another possibility is the prayer of John Chrysostom, the fourth-century bishop of Constantinople famed for his eloquence and remembered for his extraordinary courage. His prayer affirms our rationale for prayer. The line that reads, "When two or three are gathered together, you will be in the midst of them," asks for guidance as we carry the work of prayer into the world. The prayer concludes on an eschatological note: "Grant us in this world knowledge of your truth and in the age to come life everlasting." The dynamic is different from that of the General Thanksgiving, providing an alternative sense of ending. Both prayers may be said. Both were required in previous editions of the *Book of Common Prayer*, but now we can make the choice as a reflection of our theological mood.

Finally, we may conclude with one of the most ancient liturgical blessings, "Let Us Bless the Lord." This option, which also serves as one of the diaconal dismissals in the eucharistic rite, was used for centuries in the monastic Office and provides a thoughtful ending. Normally we pray for God's blessing. In this blessing, however, as at the beginning of the Eucharist, we "bless the Lord." This reminds us that blessing is not a shower of supernatural benefits— which God alone could do—nor a bestowing of favor, but a relationship. The blessing sets aside, or consecrates, in the root sense of the word, the object of the blessing. Whenever we worship, we are blessing God. And when we ask for God's blessing in return, we are not asking for special favors, for material, intellectual, or spiritual benefits, but express our willingness to be set aside, or consecrated, for God's work.

To this blessing one may add one of three appropriate verses from New Testament letters. The first, the Pauline "grace," reverses the blessing of dismissal and asks for God's blessing on us. The second is a version of the same grace, although oriented more toward the work of the Spirit. The third, like the General Thanksgiving, is eucharistic and doxological, praising the God who works in and through us. All three choices make superb final words. All three provide a definite and meaningful sense of an ending. Beyond these words, nothing further need, or should, be said.

CHAPTER THREE
Evening Prayer

*Let my prayer be set forth in your sight as incense, the lifting up of my
hands as the evening sacrifice.*

—Psalm 141:2

Christian theology, doctrine, instruction—and before all, Christian
experience—often involve deep paradox. A shameful instrument of
torture and death, the cross of Golgotha, has become a precious
object that we boldly display.[1] The creator of the cosmos, who
speaks the world into existence, has become a wordless infant.[2] And
in serving this person, we discover perfect freedom.[3] Death and
darkness are welcomed, not feared. They are blessings, not curses.

Evening Prayer and its variations—the Order of Worship for
Evening and Compline—gently reflect this last paradox. In structure, Evening Prayer is the same as Morning Prayer. The content
is sometimes like that of Morning Prayer, sometimes diametrically
different. Both Offices are full of thanksgiving, praise, Scripture,
supplication, and opportunities for formation. Both are baptismal.
In the morning, however, the dominant note is one of triumph, life
and strength, and joyful courage, even during penitential seasons.
In the evening, by contrast, the tone is subdued, quiet; the service
is about resignation, acceptance, and peace. As noted earlier, this
form of prayer is, more than other prayer, attuned to the meanings,
moods, and rhythms of chronological time. Therefore the prayers
for evening are deliberately designed to meet our (normal)
evening needs: peace and quiet, rest, restoration.

To appreciate this aspect fully, we need to recall again the attitude of the child or imagine the attitude of earliest humanity.
Nightfall for the young represents something uncertain and unsteady:
we naturally fear the dark. The fatigue we feel at the end of the
workday frightens us. Does it mean we are permanently depleted,
injured, or sick? For countless generations of humankind, moreover,
darkness brought serious dangers on four and two feet. We wonder,
at some level, whether we shall ever wake after falling asleep.

Evening Prayer acknowledges these deep, even atavistic, feelings, and enables us to accept the coming night through the Christian paradoxes that submission is mastery, service is freedom, and death is liberation. Morning Prayer is supposed to brace us in theological joy for the experience of the day; Evening Prayer, by contrast, quietly equips us for the more passive blessings of the night.

Evening Prayer accomplishes this task through the gentle, almost subliminal, insistence on themes of peace, quiet, rest, thankfulness, and reassurance. It provides the voice of the parent soothing the child to sleep. Its message is "Do not be afraid: the darkness is good for you." The theme of nocturnal illumination is also present, since Compline, not Evening Prayer, serves as the bedtime Office. Like the light described at the beginning of the Fourth Gospel, Evening Prayer offers light in the midst of darkness, which is different from pervasive daylight. Its light is the loveliness of the candle, not the glory of the sun.

As with Morning Prayer, a set of opening scriptural sentences is provided (*BCP* 115–16). But unlike the morning set, they all concern time of day: "Yours is the day, O God, yours also the night"; "Seek him who made the Pleiades and Orion, and turns deep darkness into the morning, and darkens the day into night"; "Darkness is not dark to you, O Lord; the night is as bright as the day." The theme of reassurance is clear. A particular seasonal sentence may be used if the officiant wishes to stress that aspect of time. As usual, the Office is eminently flexible.

Evening Prayer may also begin with confession. Many have found confession more useful at Evening Prayer than in the morning, since it provides an opportunity for reflection on, and for dealing with, the inevitable shortcomings of the day. No one gets through a day without sin "against God and our neighbors." Most officiants still limit its use, since daily use of confession at Evening Prayer might emphasize self-examination over peacefulness and reassurance. A common option is twice a week—Wednesdays and Fridays, for example.

Confessional themes are expressed in the ancient opening versicle for evening, Psalm 70:1: "O God, make speed to save us. O Lord, make haste to help us." The contrast with Morning Prayer is clear. In the morning, we begin with the intention of praise, in the evening with supplication for God's help and admission of our dependency. This opening sets a tone of receptivity and acceptance, of calm and stasis, that we hear throughout the Evening Office—the evening yang against the morning yin.

Next, either of the invitatory psalms for morning or a suitable hymn may be sung or said, but the classic option is a lamplighting hymn, "O Gracious Light" (Gk. *Phos hilaron*), that dates to the third century (*BCP* 118). If sung, the hymnal offers several settings in the service-music section that can be done a cappella. There are also metrical settings such as "H 36" in the 1982 hymnal.[4] In this hymn we have the theme of light in darkness—the particular beauty of an illumination that is limited. We welcome the idea as simultaneously reassuring and restful, and relate it, in a strong echo of the Fourth Gospel, to the person of Jesus Christ. We reaffirm the doxology and eucharistic note of the morning when we say, "You are worthy at all times to be praised by happy voices."

As noted above, while it contrasts in essential ways with the morning Office, Evening Prayer replicates many of its principles. The first example is the psalmody, which follows the format and principles of the morning psalms. We do not read "evening psalms" but continue with the comprehensive sequence that is the Psalter as an entirety.

The same applies to the lessons. At Evening Prayer, the third of the three daily lessons normally is read. A custom is to read one of the New Testament lessons at Evening Prayer, either Gospel or Epistle, and to switch between the two every year so as not to associate one with the Evening Office. Local and individual practicalities often dictate variations on this reading pattern. Some read two lessons at night and one in the morning, for example, or all three in one Office when that is the only option, or a fourth lesson at Evening Prayer, customarily the Old Testament reading from the following year or an extrabiblical reading. But the two-and-one pattern remains the norm. The effect is to emphasize that Morning and Evening Prayer constitute a unit, a single experience of beginning and ending the day with prayer.

The canticles return us to the unique evening themes. For although any canticle is permissible, the classic songs for evening are the suggested options: the Song of Mary and the Song of Simeon (*BCP* 119–20). The first, the Magnificat (from its Latin translation in the fifth century), is what Mary sings in conversation with Elizabeth and in response to the angel Gabriel (Luke 1:46–55). The second, *Nunc dimittis*, is the hymn the prophet Simeon sings at his first glimpse of the promised Messiah. Both are appropriate songs for the Christian individual in that they vividly express the acceptance of the person of Christ. Mary's song revives the classic Old Testament motif of reversed expectations, expressing the comeuppance of the powerful by the exaltation of the lowly and neatly paralleling the Song of Hannah in 1 Samuel. Simeon's hymn represents the Old Testament context of messianic expectation and universalism. Such expectation sees the Messiah as both the glory of Israel, the one longed for through the ages, and as a light to the nations. This is the vision of late Isaiah, wherein Yahweh is envisioned for the first time as Lord over all nations and as God of the whole cosmos.

Both songs are appropriate as evening hymns in that they reinforce the themes of peace, restfulness, resignation, and acceptance. The Song of Mary, in fact, was borrowed for these reasons from traditional Evening Offices in Western monasteries. The *Nunc dimittis* is borrowed from Compline, or bedtime prayers. Just as the *Phos hilaron* is the prayer for candle lighting, so the *Nunc* marks the time for blowing out candles. Both are powerful and lovely evening prayers.

The Baptismal Creed (*BCP* 120) is next. If said at the Morning Office the creed may be omitted in the evening, thus emphasizing the unity of the two services. Then follow the salutation and Lord's Prayer (121), for which the same considerations apply as at Morning Prayer. The first set of suffrages also duplicates the morning suffrages. The second set, however, is distinctly appropriate to Evening Prayer. Based on ancient Eastern suffrages, the second set is in litany rather than dialogue form. That is, the response is identical with each petition: "We entreat you, O Lord." Why the slightly old-fashioned word *entreat* in prayers that are deliberately contemporary? According to the Belgian student of Christian worship, Anton Baumstark, occasions of solemnity and seriousness tend to be conservative. Good Friday, for example, thus retains some of the oldest rites in the tradition, and the Paschal Vigil, which seems new and innovative to the uninitiated, in fact represents a return to a custom practically as old as Christianity itself. The slightly archaic wording may simply be another example of this principle. Whatever the source of the word *entreat*, the second set of suffrages is beautifully in tune with the associations of evening traced above. We ask that this evening be "holy, good, and peaceful," we ask for the care of angels—that our departure from this life may be in faith and fear of the Lord—and, finally, we "entrust one another and all our life to Christ," having been "bound together by [the] Holy Spirit" in the communion of saints.

As in Morning Prayer, the Collect of the Day follows, reiterating what was said in the morning. The evening collects, again offered in a set of seven to provide one for each day of the week, are again more appropriate for their time of day than their morning counterparts.

CHAPTER FOUR

The Minor Offices

Guide us waking, Lord, and guard us sleeping.
—The Book of Common Prayer

One of the five pillars of Islam is prayer, and for almost all Muslims this means the five-times-daily practice of praise and petition. The action involves prostration toward Mecca as its most outward manifestation, but also includes words remarkably similar to our Judeo-Christian prayers. Asked to explain this practice of prayer, Muslims inevitably point to the real sense of corporate strength they derive from the idea that throughout the world fellow followers of Mohammed are praying the same words at the same time.

I have always admired this Muslim practice and precept. It is deliberately intrusive by interrupting the day's business. That makes no difference to the Muslim, whose commitment to God supersedes all other commitments. The daily interruption makes for a striking public affirmation of one's theological identity, but, more important, it serves as constant reinforcement of the reality of prayer.

All Muslims, not just clerics, are bound by this rule. By contrast, the only comparable rule in Christian tradition has been that of the monastery, wherein the seven- or eightfold Office is practiced, or that of the cathedral church, which offered several Offices throughout the day. Secular Christians are encouraged for the most part simply to develop a daily prayer life on a spontaneous and informal basis. Anglicanism is, in fact, one of the only Christian traditions that does offer a twice-daily standard for individual secular Christians and for ordinary parishes.

For some individuals and parishes those two Offices will not be enough. For example, the parish group (or any group) on weekend retreat may feel the need for more frequent nonsacramental prayer. The parish in a busy neighborhood may want to offer a fuller round of Offices that accommodates parishioners, guests, and drop-ins at different hours. An individual may feel the need for more frequent prayer. Christians may feel the need for the frequent prayer that Muslims enjoy.

For the first time the current *Book of Common Prayer* has recognized these needs and provides, in addition to the twofold Morning and Evening Prayer scheme, two supplementary or "minor" Offices: an Order of Service for Noonday, and Compline. It also provides an alternative to or embellishment of Evening Prayer in the "Order of Worship for the Evening," and a set of "Daily Devotions for Individuals and Families." All of these options can potentially enrich the Office experience of groups or individuals. They are exceedingly brief and therefore useful even for the busiest of persons. They are geared on the one hand to times distinct from morning and evening, and on the other hand to private, nonparochial settings.

These smaller or "minor" Offices can serve the needs of groups meeting occasionally. They can also, naturally, meet the needs of monastic communities, which can afford a more comprehensive sanctification of time. For the first time monastic communities can base their entire Office work on the *Book of Common Prayer* and not import forms from elsewhere or invent forms of their own (as explained below). For individuals, on the other hand, the minor Offices require only willingness to devote a brief period at midday and bedtime to prayer and praise. Certainly these Offices are not "for everybody" in the same way as Morning and Evening Prayer. But they are useful for more people than are currently aware of them. My own experience, observations, and understanding of the minor Offices are that they become useful to individuals and groups for certain periods, then fall aside as other pressures make them less viable. That is one reason, I believe, they are optional. The Daily Office in its twofold form of Morning and Evening Prayer feels binding in a way that the minor Offices do not.

That twofold pattern lies behind the more elaborate structure of the monastic Office. Although, as we have seen, the many Offices in monastic practice were often explained as a fulfillment of the psalmist's statement that "seven times a day do I praise God," this was almost certainly not their origin. Rather, the seven- or eightfold Office simply spun out of the twofold Office in order to meet the felt need for more frequent prayer. That is why the minor Offices resemble, in small, Morning and Evening Prayer.

Order of Service for Noonday (BCP 103–7). Sandwiched between Morning and Evening Prayer, this service follows the outline of the two longer prayer services: opening rite, psalm, Scripture lessons, prayers. From this outline, however, the optional enrichments have all been omitted. There is no invitatory to introduce the psalmody. There are no canticles to set off the lesson. There is no Creed. There is no litany. The single benediction is all that is left of the closing rite. Suggested psalms and readings are abbreviated.

Unless the Office is deliberately extended for some reason—by a long meditation on the lesson, for example—it will take less than five minutes to pray. The reason is not only practical, although it is true that the Offices are useful for busy people at odd moments. The short length is also true to the history of the minor Offices. Our Order of Service for Noonday is in fact an amalgam of the monastic Offices of Terce, Sext, and None, prayed in many monasteries at the third, sixth, and ninth hours of the day. *Noon*, the modern word descended from *none*, meant "midafternoon," or about three o'clock. The three psalms and the four collects suggested for noonday reflect this fact. Collect One is most appropriate for about nine in the morning, the second for 12 noon, and so on. But this arrangement again is highly flexible. What we have in the noonday service is a "daytime" Office, appropriate anytime between the first Office of the day and the first Office of the evening.

A monastic community is free to develop the minor Offices into traditional Prime, Sext, and None forms and to pray them at regular hours. They are likewise free to develop a continuous reading schedule for the lesson. The rubric deliberately appoints "one of the following, or some other suitable passage of scripture." They are also free to develop "free intercessions." Individuals, similarly, are free to develop practices based on these forms for regular hours. On the other hand, any group meeting intermittently or on a one-time basis may read the Office as is, using the appropriate readings and collects. A group meeting at 9 A.M. might find it helpful to pray for the direction of the Holy Spirit as in Collect One. A group meeting at noon may find it refreshing to reflect on the fact that "at this hour" Jesus hung upon the cross, or that at noonday Paul was called to be an apostle. A group meeting at 4 P.M. may find comfort in the fourth collect, which in its prayer for peace and unity begins to anticipate the irenic qualities of Evening Prayer discussed above.

*Order of Worship for the Evening (*BCP *109–14)*. This is the anomaly among Offices. It is the only variation of the Office designed "for suitable occasions," as the rubric suggests; in other words, unlike every other Office, it is not designed for daily use. It is included in the Office section of the prayer book because it is a variation of the Office. It is not, however, Evening Prayer with added elements.

When we looked at origins for the Office, I made the generalization that it derived primarily from synagogue services and personal devotions, while the Eucharist derived from temple worship and family rites. The Order for Evening is the exception to that generalization. It is based, ultimately, on the weekly Jewish family service, which began (and for many still begins) with the ritual of lamplighting, followed by psalmody and lessons. Christianity assimilated the service, making it part of cathedral practice in many places, but it was eclipsed gradually by Evening Prayer or vespers.

The current prayer book offers the service as an occasional variation on the Evening Office. The question as to what a "suitable occasion" might be is left to the community. One possibility, honoring the service's historical source, might be to offer it once a week. Another possibility would be to use it on special occasions when visitors are expected—at meetings, for example, or ecumenical gatherings. Yet another possibility would be when supper follows as part of the evening's activities—an option that again recognizes the origins of the service.

The Order for the Evening has a practical value that should not go unmentioned. It has much in common with another ritual that the current prayer book restores and that many parishes have discovered in recent decades: the great Vigil of Easter (*BCP* 284ff.), a spectacular rite, which for the early church was the most important observance in the Christian year. Offering the Order for Evening several times throughout the year can help worshipers become more proficient at the service of light that opens both this Order and the vigil. Besides the practical matter of lighting candles, itself a serious consideration, practice helps us to be more psychologically and spiritually ready for the dramatic opening rite of the vigil.

Compline (BCP *127–35*). People who have practiced the Offices for a while will often say that the Office they like best is Compline. This seems strange at first. After all, Compline is one of the "little Offices," an abbreviated version of Morning and Evening Prayer. Like the noonday Office, it is rarely used on a daily basis outside of monastic communities. It is instead prayed occasionally, at the end of an evening parish event, for example, or when people are together on retreat.

While Evening Prayer intends to help us embrace the blessings of the evening, Compline takes this one more step, gently urging us to welcome sleep. It is, in fact, a classic bedtime prayer. All the childlike implications of that, and the natural human associations of death and sleep, are present in this lovely last Office of the day.

Daily Devotions for Individuals and Families (BCP *136–40*). We now come to the final option in the Daily Office section of the *Book of Common Prayer.* In one sense, this option simply continues prayer-book tradition. A set of daily private prayers has always been provided, consistent with the original Anglican impulse to extend the practice of prayer beyond the church building.

As noted from the outset, however, the regular Daily Office is suitable for private or family use, as well as for parish practice, and the current prayer book makes that clearer than ever before. What, then, is the purpose of this set of four devotional forms? If anyone can pray the Office anywhere, why include this version?

The Daily Devotions serve the same purpose for the Office as the Order for Celebrating the Holy Eucharist (*BCP* 400) provides for that sacrament: a less structured, less formal alternative that still preserves the essential elements of the rite. Consider the form suggested for morning (*BCP* 137), for example. Obviously, it is a version of Morning Prayer. But all embellishments, all inessential options—no matter how edifying—have been eliminated. The form consists of a psalm, a reading from Scripture, the Lord's

Prayer, and a collect—the backbone of the Office. As the first rubric concerning the forms states, "These devotions follow the basic structure of the Daily Office of the Church" (*BCP* 136).

The method of abbreviating the Office can be easily seen by looking at the psalm portion of the service. Instead of the opening versicle, an invitatory psalm with or without antiphons, and a full psalm provided in the regular Office, a selection from a single psalm is suggested. The segment is from Psalm 51, a classic morning psalm, capturing something of the main purpose of the normal Office sequence—which, as we saw, is praise and orientation of self. The normal fullness of expression is eliminated along with the day-to-day exploration of the Psalter, but the essential element is still present.

Within the form of the service several options are listed. Silence may follow the reading, canticles or hymns added, the Baptismal Creed said, and extemporaneous intercessions "for ourselves and others" voiced. The rubrics that precede the forms remind us that we are free to use the daily lectionary for the psalm and readings, if we like, or the Collect of the Day or any collect "appointed in the Daily Offices" (*BCP* 136). The more we follow these suggestions, the more the Daily Devotions will start to resemble the usual Daily Office. In fact, if we continue by adding a second reading, an invitatory, and canticles after the readings, we end up with the full Office. We would thus retrace the Office's historical development.

That is the reason these forms still appear in the *Book of Common Prayer*, and that is why they have been included (for the first time) in the opening section of the book. In the 1928 prayer book, as in previous editions, "Forms of Prayer to Be Used in Families" were printed near the back, between the catechism and the Articles of Religion—a random gathering of elements suggesting an afterthought. The prayers for use in the morning, for example, to be said by "the Master or Mistress" of the household, also exhibited a random structure. They began with the Lord's Prayer, specified four dedicatory prayers, and listed a collect as an option. In other words, the service consisted of five randomly listed prayers with the possibility of a sixth, without psalmody or readings. In no sense was this a variation of Morning Prayer, which then, as always, opened the prayer book.

Instead of eliminating these devotions as redundant or relegating them to an appendix like the "Historical Documents," the current prayer book has transformed them into a streamlined variation on the Office. From a practical standpoint, they are useful when there is no time for the full Office, even in its simplest form, as in emergencies or when one is ill. The Daily Devotions guide individuals through a minute or so of serious, genuine prayer. They can also serve as a gentle introduction to the Daily Office for those who find the full forms complex, difficult, or time-consuming. If the Office lectionary and Collect of the Day are used—which I have found to be the best option—then none of our principles of sequence and variety is compromised.

Most important, the dynamic of the Daily Office—its powerful sequence of praise, listening, and petition—is preserved in small in these Daily Devotions. Their obvious simplicity and their equally obvious flexibility make them a perfect complement to the full Office in its various forms. That is what they are for—not to replace the Office, not to serve as a regular alternative, but to stand in as a special variation of the Office itself, appropriate for almost everyone at some time.

CHAPTER FIVE

A Theology of
the Daily Office

You are God: we praise you.
—The Book of Common Prayer

The Daily Office is dramatic. I do not mean this in the popular sense of vivid or stirring, but in a specific and technical sense. It is very much a daily drama. Prayer is, at the most basic level, conversation, and drama is structured, meaningful dialogue. The greatest dramatic works—Shakespeare, the Greek tragedians, the Book of Job—express virtually everything through dialogue alone. The Daily Office allows for both halves of the dialogue and the full context for a daily conversation with God. And just as drama reveals character, the Daily Office expresses a theology.

This expression is especially appropriate for a prayer-book service. Basic to Anglicanism since its inception has been the ancient principle of *lex orandi, lex credendi*—"the law of prayer is the law of belief." Our theology may be expressed in many other ways—through doctrinal pronouncements, homiletics, theological treatises—but a central feature of our tradition has always been to express theology in and through our worship life, our prayer book, and our liturgy. This is a holistic principle central to the denominational ethos. Not only do we believe what we pray—presumably everyone does that—but we pray what we believe.

At the same time, this form of worship has a practical, common-sense importance. Although the sacraments may have a greater theological weight, the Office, by virtue of its daily aspect, must have theological persuasiveness. Anything reinforced daily, we have suggested, is bound to have profound cumulative effects on the human consciousness. Then again, we must consider that Anglicanism gives unique prominence to the Daily Office. It is placed first in the *Book of Common Prayer*. The central text is referred to as "Common Prayer," which, as noted at the outset, refers properly to the Office only. All this reminds us to take the theology of the Office seriously.

What, then, is the theology of the Daily Office?

Doxology and Eucharist in the Office

The Daily Office is doxological and eucharistic, not in the sacramental sense but in the root sense of these words. It begins and ends, as we have seen, in acts of praise, and is suffused throughout with thanksgiving. From the initial prayer, "Lord, open our lips, and our mouth shall proclaim your praise,"[1] through the invitatory and psalms, the Lord's Prayer, and the dismissal, "let us bless the Lord," the dominant theme is joyful praise. Sometimes the praise is muted, and many other themes may be expressed as well, but praise is unmistakably present every day.

Acts of praise in the Office should never be treated as pro forma gestures, as liturgical decoration, or as verbal padding. Doxology, more than any other element, is what the Daily Office is about; in a larger sense, it is what prayer is about. That is why, no matter what other elements may appear, doxology, the praise of God, will always be expressed first and foremost.

This suggests a theological kinship with the Eucharist. The word *Eucharist* means both thanksgiving and praise.[2] The Office incorporates these elements, which makes sense if we think of the Office and the Eucharist not as separate entities, or as different services that the church offers, but as different moments in the same conversation. We often think that we are having an "ongoing" conversation with a friend or loved one, especially when we discuss a topic important to both of us. That is exactly what happens in our prayer life. It is an ongoing conversation with God and is never suspended. The Office, the Eucharist, other services, sporadic, private moments of prayerful communication, and spiritual reading are all moments in that continuous conversation.

Since there exists, in any conversation with individuals important to us, a grammar or even etiquette of approach, so it is with God. In the Eucharist and the Office, the two most formal forms of communication listed above, that etiquette is most important. The etiquette demands thanksgiving and praise as the most appropriate responses of creature to creator.

The Office and the Eucharist are, thus, complementary in their doxological nature, but do contrast in the placement of the main eucharistic element. In the Eucharist, the main element is the eucharistic prayer, which is placed in climactic position at or near the end of the event. In the Office, the doxological focus—as opposed to the theme of praise, which is found throughout—is the psalm, which opens and sets the tone for the whole service. As we have seen, the use of the invitatory guarantees an opening of praise and thanksgiving. Even when the appointed psalm laments, frets, whines, or even despairs, the invitatory soars, and the one praying "from sullen earth sings hymns at heaven's gate."

The climactic position in the Office is that of the collect, which, in its classic form, is also eucharistic. It generally offers praise and thanksgiving for God's grace as manifested in the past and present. The petitions gather around the collect and are focused rather than random. The idea is not simply to offer a checklist of concerns to which God should attend, but to cooperate with the providential goodness of God by sharing concerns with God.

Finally, in this predominantly eucharistic emphasis, the Daily Office reflects a tendency seen throughout the current *Book of Common Prayer:* the return to the theology of the early church. This aspect particularly suggests the influence of the three "Cappadocians": Gregory of Nazianzus, Gregory of Nyssa, and Basil the Great. These were the most eminent of the theologians who worked out their thought in the wake of the first ecumenical Council of Nicaea, in 325. They were concerned with matters such as the Incarnation, the distinction between the persons of the Trinity, and the identity of the Holy Spirit. But through their theological work, they also evinced a profound sense of Eucharist as humankind's proper and natural response to God. This lies behind Basil's great Eucharistic Prayer (which lies behind our Eucharistic Prayer D), but also informs the entire *Book of Common Prayer—* beginning with the Office.

Triumphal Christology in the Office

In harmony with this first aspect of praise, the Office expresses a triumphal model of the work of Christ. That is, the view of the atonement implicit throughout the Office, and compatible with it, understands Christ's death as, ultimately, a victory over sin and death. Twentieth-century theologian Gustav Aulen described such thinking as the classic *Christus Victor* theology well represented in the thought and spirituality of the undivided church of the first several centuries, wherein Christ's work of suffering, death, resurrection, and ascension were understood primarily as acts of victory or triumph. In place of a model that focuses on the pathetic sufferings of Jesus, "paying the price" we cannot pay (the medieval model), or on personal salvation (the evangelical model) or on Jesus' ethical teachings (the humanist model), this Christology depicts Christ as victorious, reigning in heaven or even from the cross itself.

This vision is most clearly expressed in the Easter invitatory, the *Pascha nostrum*. For fifty days each year, the person who prays the Daily Office starts the day with this awesome hymn of victory, one of the most ancient poems in the Christian tradition. Its spirit also suffuses the canticles—they are all songs of victory at one level or another, praising God for victories past, present, and/or to come—and many of the daily and weekly collects in the prayer book. Such theology is also implicit in the Baptismal Creed.

This theological aspect has been made clearer by revisions to the prayer book. Previous versions of the Daily Office, still borrowing from late medieval forms, placed more emphasis on the propitiatory aspects of Christ's work as they emphasized the penitential aspects of our spirituality. The current prayer book has eliminated—or, in some instances, made optional—almost all of the later medieval additions that obscured the more ancient emphasis on *Christus Victor*.

The Holy Spirit in the Office

The Holy Spirit is a clear and present reality throughout the Office. It is therefore, in the classic sense, a pentecostal form for prayer.

I have stressed throughout that one function of the Office is to teach us to pray: not to memorize words, but how to structure our thoughts toward God and how to express them. We begin the day with the words, "Lord, open our lips, / and our mouth shall proclaim your praise," asking for this ability.

This process outlines what happens at Pentecost. However we interpret the event, it clearly involves the giving of the Holy Spirit, the "descent of the dove," and the new apostolic ability to express prayer. What amazes the onlookers is not the strangeness sometimes associated with Pentecost but the apostles' intelligibility—the amazing thing is that everybody can understand them.

The Spirit sanctifies the tongue and human words, a sanctification that also refers to the mysterious opening words of Genesis, in which the Spirit of the Lord Yahweh hovers over the primal waters before the great act of verbal creation. By inviting God into all aspects of everyday life, the Office, in its humility, calls down the Holy Spirit.

Incarnation in the Office

The incarnational nature of the Office is implied in that it takes place daily. I do not refer specifically to the Incarnation of Christ, but to incarnation in general—to ours, as well as his. Anything done daily is incarnational. I have noted, at the anthropological level, that we exercise stewardship of the flesh daily. By *flesh* I mean more than a synonym for skin, that is, the envelope of cells that holds the body together. The biblical word for *flesh* refers to the texture and content of our human experience, which is decidedly humble and mundane. That is why I deliberately have tried throughout to employ the most down-to-earth comparisons in explaining aspects of the Office. Comparisons have been made to washing, eating, and sleeping. Every human being "knows" that these are incarnational responsibilities, and the Office is like these daily events.

I have called the Lord's Prayer "paradigmatic" for the Daily Office, in that it establishes the theme for all the intercessions that follow. The Lord's Prayer is quintessentially incarnational, with its central petition of "give us today our daily bread." No more creaturely, more physical, more dependent petition can be uttered or imagined, and we put it at the heart of our prayer.

The concerns we express in the Daily Office again affirm its incarnational nature. Because it is daily and because of its intimacy, no matter how large the assembly, the Office seems to invite and to validate the expression of the most personal concerns. People pray for help with parking tickets and runny noses, pop quizzes and household chores, minor aches and pains, tiny interpersonal problems and irritations—things they often feel less inclined to express (vocally) in the Eucharist. This again is the incarnational aspect at work, reminding us that God knows about these concerns—not only rationally but experientially, in the person of one who was tempted as we are. We are reminded that Jesus, the human being, knew not only the agony of Golgotha and Gethsemane, but also the agony of ordinary ennui, mild anxiety, and the common cold. Otherwise, he cannot be said to have experienced what we experience. Indeed, for many people, the occasional heroic triumph may be easier than the day-to-day managing of the thousand natural shocks the flesh is heir to. The Office helps us keep all in perspective. It helps us cope, and that is a great blessing.

The distinction drawn at the outset between the two human experiences of time, between seasonal time (*kairos*) and clock time (*chronos*), applies. *Kairos* time, sacramental time, is the inbreaking of the transcendent; it is "vertical" and can occur at any time. Chronological time is immanent, "horizontal"; it is ongoing, constant. Chronological time is incarnational time, and the Office is the perfect way to mark it. We mark seasons through the sacraments, preeminently through Eucharist, but we "tell time" through the Office.

Scripture in the Office

That the Daily Office is scriptural should be clear by this point. First, like most of the services in the *Book of Common Prayer*, the text of the Office is largely derived from Scripture. About 75 percent of its sentences and phrases are direct biblical quotation. The Office as it has developed over the centuries presents a dynamic use of the Bible. This is Scripture being put to use, prayed Scripture. It makes Scripture a part of one's daily life in a more compelling way than "studying" passages in an intellectual—or in a highly emotional—way.

Second, the Office encourages what we normally think of as "Bible study." As we have seen, the lectionary supplies a daily measure of Scripture, generally geared to the Christian year, always substantial enough to serve as food for thought throughout the day, never so long as to be burdensome. Most people who practice the Office for any length of time will find themselves involved with Scripture in a way they have never known. Many will begin to ask questions usually thought of as the province of scholars, concerning the source, motivation, and result of scriptural sayings. Most Christians would assent to Paul's notion that Scripture is "profitable." The Daily Office challenges and ultimately affirms this notion.

Third, the concept of the Office is itself scriptural. It is a biblical idea, based on several biblical ideas and precedents. A twice-daily pattern of formal prayer is reflected several times in biblical history, notably in the case of Jesus and the apostles. They pray at the normal temple hours, and their private prayer lives seem structured around the time of day. The Office is biblical in that it is structured around psalmody, the original prayer book being the Book of Psalms. Indeed it resembles the rest of the Bible, which quotes psalms on virtually every page. Finally, and perhaps most important, the Office follows scriptural norms for petitionary prayer, as seen in the Our Father. The idea of daily petition is one of the most profound themes throughout Scripture, and the Office serves as a catalyst for such prayer.

Baptismal Themes in the Office

The Daily Office is baptismal in nature. Christians today are in a better position than in previous eras to appreciate the weight of this theology. The late twentieth century has seen the recovery of the ancient primacy of baptism. One of the two sacraments definitively given by Jesus, baptism was, in the crucial, normative, protean era of the church, the great rite of initiation, renewal, rebirth, transformation, and victory. It was the outward and visible sign that the individual shared with Christ in his resurrection. It was also the symbol of his or her entry into the Christian family. Centuries of trivialization had reduced this powerful reality to the private blessing of a new baby, but now we have begun to restore the sacrament to its full weight.

The recovery of the Office parallels and reinforces this larger development. The paradigmatic Office, as hinted throughout this book, is Morning Prayer. The other Offices are parallels and extensions. Morning Prayer establishes the structure and spiritual tone for the day, and, in theme, its fixed content is the same as the baptismal ceremony, incorporating ideas of rebirth, new beginnings, and victory.

The Baptismal Creed is always repeated at least once a day in the Office, reinforcing our sense of baptismal identity. Repetition of the Apostles' Creed is also a daily reaffirmation of one's baptismal vows, since, in tripartite form, it reflects the content of the baptismal examination. The Apostles' Creed, as opposed to the corporate Nicene Creed, is the individual's credo, reinforcing the paradoxically individual nature of the Office.

The Creed is also a distillation of God's revelation of God's self, as we understand it. The lectionary provides, over twenty-four months, the discursive, comprehensive reading of that same revelation—the eighty books that constitute Scripture. The readings, in other words, gradually set before us that which the Creed summarizes. The two work together to reform and inform and to establish our Christian identity. Just as the earliest Christians spent at least two years in the study of Scripture in preparation for baptism, so we now spend every two years gradually reading it in the context of the Office.

The baptismal covenant also involves clear ethical demands: we are to seek Christ in all persons, loving our neighbor as ourselves. The Office reflects these ideas throughout. In its intercessory concerns we are reminded of our duties and responsibilities toward neighbor and the rest of creation. The act of praying intercessory prayers is one form of living out and fulfilling the baptismal promises, for we inevitably pray in a way that expresses love for the neighbor. The dismissal, moreover, reinforces this idea, urging and challenging us to fulfill the implications of the Office through service.

I have stressed at several points that, in its theology, the Office is compatible with the Eucharist—indeed, complementary. In fact, many of the same points about theological underpinnings could be made in a study of the Eucharist. The latter, however, is not nearly so "biblical" as the Office, since the Eucharist does not contain as much biblical quotation. It is, rather, made up largely of postbiblical material. Eucharistic Prayers B, C, and D were composed in the first four centuries of Christian history, and Prayer A is based on medieval prayers. The Office contains comparatively less of this later traditional material.

Yet both prayer forms profoundly express the incarnational aspects of the faith, its baptismal nature, its spirituality, and, above all, the theology of triumph. They speak the same theological language; even the "tone" seems consistent. In part, this is because of intentional theological unity. The victory of Christ is praised at all times, and at no point do we hear that "Jesus died for your sins." The Office is part of the theological integrity that the current prayer book deliberately expresses.

I suggested another reason for this unity above. Omissions made in creating the current prayer book have affected the entire theological picture, not just the *Christus Victor* aspect. The late medieval vision of deep personal penitence as the central reality of spiritual life infested English prayer books ever since the books' sixteenth-century origins. For the first time, it has been possible to identify these influences and to eliminate them. The result has been a much older, and more positive, theological vision. The current *Book of Common Prayer* more than any earlier edition finds its roots in the theology of the earliest Christian centuries.

CHAPTER SIX

The Spirituality of the Daily Office

He has… filled the hungry with good things.
　　　　　　　　—Psalm 107:9

Spirituality is one of those frustratingly flexible words whose meaning seems obvious to everyone, but that seems to be used by each person in a slightly different way. Does it mean "having to do with the Holy Spirit"? In theology proper, the word is sometimes used that way. That would, however, make *spirituality* almost synonymous with *theology* or *religion*. Perhaps it means "having to do with the inner life of the individual," which seems to be an important contemporary sense of the word. But that would also be the meaning of *psychological*. How is spirituality to be distinguished? Does it simply mean "the intangible life of humanity, as opposed to the material"? The secular media use the word to mean exactly that.

I use the word *spirituality* in the title of this chapter in a somewhat restricted and rather traditional Christian sense. I use the word to indicate the character and content of the individual devotional life, insofar as it can be discussed and delimited. In the sixteenth and seventeenth centuries, this was called *religion* as distinct from *theology*. The latter was what a person believed, the content of his or her faith; the former was one's response to that belief in prayer, meditation, and charity. Such practice is today what "spirituality" involves for most people interested in the faith. In theological seminaries, for example, courses in spirituality involve these pragmatic issues.

I make these distinctions simply because, by any of the three broader definitions above, this entire book is about "spirituality." Any consideration of Christian prayer naturally concerns the inner life of human beings, incorporates awareness of the Holy Spirit, and emphasizes the nonmaterial aspects of experience.[1] This book is offered as a contribution to spirituality of this type, which is more accurate than labeling the book a work on "ascesis" or "devotion" or "liturgical scholarship," although all these disciplines, I hope, have informed it.

In this chapter, however, I am specifically concerned with *spirituality* in its limited sense, and how the Office expresses, suggests, and invites a practical spirituality, a *religio*. In another era, I probably would have labeled this chapter "The Religion of the Office," just as Sir Thomas Browne called his essay on his personal spirituality "Religio Medici" ("the religion of a physician"). But that would be misleading today, suggesting to most people a theological discussion rather than an individual practice. That is why this chapter follows the chapter on the theology of the Office. Spirituality is, among other things, a response to the nature of one's theological framework, and a discussion of the spirituality of the Office similarly follows as a response to its theology.

For centuries, the practice of formal, daily prayer—of which the Daily Office is a principal type—has been a cornerstone of Christian spirituality. It was, in some form at least, central to the formation and nurture of many great teachers and theologians, mystics and visionaries, pilgrims and solitaries, counselors and spiritual directors. From the apostolic fathers and mothers to the present, many Christians have prayed the Daily Office or comparable daily devotion. For countless Christian leaders, healers, teachers, and pilgrims, the Office has represented daily bread.

It is the Office's daily aspect that makes it easy to overlook its importance. We tend to notice the terrible beauty of the visions of a Julian of Norwich, the biblicism that informs the creative erudition of Bede, the brilliance of Anselm or Bonaventure or Thomas Cranmer, or the poetic genius of George Herbert or John Donne. The daily prayer life they all had in common, the steady nourishment through psalm, lesson, Creed, and canticle, is not as evident. They did not talk or write about such practice, but took it for granted. Lady Julian left us a handful of visions that she received. We tend to forget the thousands of days when she saw no visions, but heard the word instead in lessons and psalms.

The exploration of the Daily Office thus far should have established its historical importance, liturgical strengths, theological depths, and scriptural bases. These ideas have proven simple to establish. The spirituality of the Office, by contrast, is complex and open-ended in its possibilities. The Office's inherent flexibility makes it compatible with various spiritual traditions. I discuss three compatible traditions: Benedictine monasticism, that of the desert fathers, and non-Christian practices such as Zen.

First, the *Benedictine path* represents a harmonious complement to the Daily Office. After all, it was above all from the Benedictine forms of the monastic Office that Cranmer and other sixteenth-century Reformers borrowed in making Morning and Evening Prayer. Our Daily Office may, in fact, usefully be thought of as a telescoping of the eightfold Benedictine Offices into two, as suggested in chapter 1. This change intended to make the blessings of the Monastic Office available to every baptized person, rather than to the small minority who have the monastic vocation.

But there is more to Benedictine life than recitation of the eightfold Office, and more to Benedictine spirituality than time spent in Chapel of Choir. Benedict offered his *Rule* as a comprehensive approach to the totality of human experience. It is, in a word, a *Rule* of life, and its spirit is meant to permeate the lives of the monks who adhere to it. It governs everything from table manners to business matters, but the *Rule*'s basic principle is simple and familiar. Its model is the human family, and the ordinary implications of that fact have always characterized the Benedictine experience at its best.

The Daily Office is in harmony with that spirit. Praying the Office can form part of the rule of life for any baptized person, whatever their vocation and mission. It can form the centerpiece of life, just as it has been the centerpiece not only of Benedictine but of other families of monastic practice for centuries. It sanctifies, in a brief and simple way, the daily experience of the Christian person who takes seriously what Presiding Bishop Frank Griswold has called "intentional discipleship." Just as the eightfold Office structures the day of the Benedictine monk, so the twofold Office sanctifies the busy day of the secular Christian. That chronological character noted from the outset of this book guarantees such sanctification. The Office begins and ends the day on a note of baptismal identity and with deliberate acts of thanksgiving and self-dedication.

The Office also lends itself to the simple yet profound practice that the Benedictines developed early in their history. This practice involves spiritual "recollection" to extend awareness of the Office throughout the day. It involves fixing the mind on a prayer, an image suggested by a reading, or small fragment of the text read during the lessons and recalling the image or words periodically throughout the day.

As medievalist Dom Jean Leclercq explains in his classic study of Benedictine spirituality, *The Love of Learning and the Desire for God*, this is how many monastics integrated spirituality into the rest of their experience. It enabled them to "take the Office with them." The practice can offer the same benefits to the modern secular practitioner of the Daily Office, helping to make Morning and Evening Prayer emotionally and practically helpful. It is in fact the basis of all the more specific and more modern approaches to hearing the lectionary outlined in chapter 2, but is more than that. The Benedictine practice works against the fragmented, alienated quality many contemporary persons feel.

Second, the Office is compatible with an even older school of spirituality, that of the *desert*, which, like the Benedictine school, is enjoying a certain vogue among contemporary searchers. Numerous people have become aware of the *Sayings of the Desert Fathers*, for example, the collections of short, challenging stories and proverbs attributed to these early spiritual explorers. Perhaps the fathers' existential situation seems eerily parallel to ours. The early desert monastics were serious believers who sought refuge from the distractions of a rapidly modernizing world, from the confusions of a bewildering religious pluralism, and from the complacency of the newly established church—impulses many of us can understand.[2]

Like the Benedictines, the desert pilgrims sought an intrusive spirituality. Almost by definition, their lives became saturated with the faith. The difference between the two traditions, however, lies in the practitioners' lifestyles. The Benedictine *Rule* provides an inherently familiar and comforting spiritual practice while the desert way offers extreme challenge. Desert pilgrims were vulnerable to powerful spiritual assaults, and spiritual protection became all the more necessary. A key text became the passage in Ephesians concerning the "armor of God" (6:10–17). They became interested in the protective presence of angels and sensed danger from demons and evil spirits, along with the equally vivid dangers of carnivorous animals.

This dangerous milieu and concomitant need for protection gave rise to a spirituality of vigilance and preparedness. The Offices prayed by these earliest of monastics—who preceded Benedict by several centuries—were characterized by flexibility and diversity; by serious and uninterrupted readings of Scripture in course; and by constant, comprehensive use of the Psalms. The desert fathers never exhibit the beautiful liturgical uniformity we find among the Benedictines, but we do find them devouring Scripture and singing psalms.

One ancient devotional technique appears in the writings of John Cassian, one of the compilers of the desert sayings whose main endeavor was to bring their way of life to other serious Christians throughout the world. The technique focuses on a psalm phrase, such as "be still and know that I am God" or "my soul for God in silence waits," and makes that phrase a Christian mantra that can be prayed over and over in the heart. This is the source of all later schools of devotion—such as the use of the Jesus prayer in the *Way of the Pilgrim*—that use such internal repetition as a means of getting beyond the rational, intellectual, and even the emotional levels to areas of deep spirituality.

This is superficially similar to the Benedictine technique in its use of repetition and in its focus on a single phrase, although Benedictines use the entire lectionary while Cassian commends the Psalms only. The two techniques are very different, however, in that the Benedictine method tries to comprehend and understand the text in as many ways as possible—to extract spiritual nutrient—while the desert method seeks to exclude surface senses of the words, to let the words penetrate to the heart of the matter and to the heart of the person praying.

The Daily Office, in its current prayer-book incarnation, is in harmony with the desert spirituality as well. It is by far the most flexible version of the Daily Office ever offered, and is adaptable to the needs of the individual. It is sequential in its reading plan. Scripture truly adheres to the person praying the contemporary Office. And the Psalter is at the heart of it. As we have seen, the Office itself is in many ways a web of scriptural texts, and no texts are better represented than the Psalms, which are not only read through more often than any other book of the Bible but also serve as the seams and hinges that hold the Office together.

In a larger sense, anyone who feels a spiritual kinship with the desert experience, who appreciates spiritual danger and challenge, can find comfort and strength in praying the Office. I have suggested the triumphal, doxological quality of the Office's theological emphases above. That quality gives it a bracing, exhilarating character. The need for continual affirmation in a pluralistic and confusing world is addressed not only by the continual reading of the scriptural record, but also by the regular reaffirmation of the content of Christian faith and by the renewal of baptismal identity with the daily Creed. The need for deliverance from evil is also constantly addressed through the Lord's Prayer and other intercessions.

Third, the Office is compatible with *non-Christian traditions*—an important consideration for many contemporary Christians and others. I have claimed from the outset a comprehensiveness for the Daily Office, an ecumenical compatibility. I noted in the introductory chapter that many Western Christians in recent decades have discovered and found themselves drawn to Eastern expressions of spirituality, to Hindu and Buddhist schools of philosophy, ascetic practices, and meditative techniques that once seemed merely exotic and quaint to Occidentals. Expressions such as Christian Zen, Christian Yoga, and Zen Catholicism have appeared during the past several decades, suggesting a spiritual ecumenism to fulfill the prediction of historian Arnold Toynbee, who foresaw a synthesis of Western and Eastern spirituality replacing the exclusive, departmentalized traditional religions of the world.

With this cross-cultural synthesis the Daily Office is, again, harmonious. For example, the Zen practice of *zazen*, which is in a sense "nothing but" sitting in silent mindfulness, is completely compatible with the practice of the Office. The two reinforce each other. I know and have known Christian monastics, for example, who practice both concomitantly. The Office encourages unlimited periods of silence, as we have seen. There is nothing inconsistent, for anyone who has the time, in practicing *zazen* in the context of Morning and Evening Prayer. All that Zen practice requires, externally speaking, is a period spent sitting in silence. That is exactly what the Daily Office encourages as well.

Zen concerns itself with life in the present moment, without the anxious distractions of past and future that normally plague our awareness. Techniques often advocated for Zen beginners, such as counting inhalations, are catalysts to this end, focal points in the spiritual path. The object is, paradoxically, to be without object. The aim is not to aim, and thereby to reach the target.

The Daily Office encourages a similar vision in its own simplicity, brevity, and sanctification of the ordinary. No sacramental transformation is expected; rather, the idea is a daily sameness, a simple consistency, that leads to the appreciation of the sacredness of ordinary existence. Psalms are read, lessons heard, prayers offered, silence kept. This is all that "happens" in the Daily Office, and, like the practice of Zen, it can look simplistic and even mind-numbing to the observer. Both practices find their transcendence within the ordinary, their holiness within the human. They can be practiced during the same session and, eventually, they can be practiced at the same time.

The Daily Office in its flexibility is compatible, then, with several classic schools of spirituality, and with any number of devotional practices. In and of itself, it expresses a unique spiritual character. In and of itself, it constitutes a school of spirituality, a way of devotion. This fact is inherent in the Office's distinguishing characteristics.

First, that the Office, by design and by nature, takes place daily is instructive. Recall at this point my initial remarks on the nature of daily activities. One feature they have in common is that they are never options. We have no choice but to do them. We do not ask ourselves, "Should I eat food today?" or "Should I sleep tonight?" unless extraordinary emergencies force us to ask such questions. In general we do not regard daily tasks as particularly onerous. Unless we are injured or upset, we do not think of getting dressed as difficult or painful. We scarcely think of it as a "task" at all.

This is true even for tasks that are initially difficult. The person who has trained the body by running three miles every day, who has trained the mind by translating Greek or by working mathematical problems, or who has acquired musical talent by daily practice does not perceive these activities as difficult. Such activities are by definition painful and forbidding initially, but are no longer painful once they are part of daily life. The fact is that, at a stage we no longer may remember, getting dressed and eating at the table were challenging tasks. Nothing practiced daily, in other words, is hard for the practitioner—however difficult it might be for anyone else.

The issue is not one of mastery. It is a matter of time and structure. Anything done on a daily basis becomes part of the texture of life. We come not simply to accept but to welcome it. Some feel that such activity regiments us, but, on the contrary, anyone who has developed a "discipline" knows that it is paradoxically liberating. Calling it a "discipline" is fundamentally misleading, since the connotations of that word are difficulty and strain.

This is perhaps the best way to understand the unique spirituality of the Daily Office. At first, like any daily task, it is difficult, although difficult in a different way than solving a mathematical problem. Once the technical skill of "doing" it is mastered—once, in other words, one understands how to choose collects, how to use the lectionary, and so on—it may seem dry and tedious, "the same old thing every day." But it is not dull once we learn to notice the powerful sequence of readings, the alternation of psalm moods, and so on. In this, it replicates the learning curve of the examples above.

Once these initial stages are completed, however, the Office becomes easy—or, better, the word *easy* no longer makes sense. We do not think of getting dressed as "easy," but as an unquestioned part of our experience. It has taken on "a life of its own." For the few minutes it takes to pray it, the Office becomes an animate presence.

The fundamental difference between the practice of the Daily Office and these other examples is that the Office truly does involve an animate presence, a conscious, personal Other. One reason that I have stressed the informal character of the Office has been to point toward this aspect of its spirituality. The Office is a brief, intimate, daily conversation with God, a way of saying "good morning" and "good evening" to God and of sharing serious concerns as well as formal conversational pleasantries.

In this the Office provides a helpful complement to sacramental worship, which is by nature much more formal and more involved with the transcendent aspect of God. This contrast has implications for individual spirituality. I have stressed the complementary aspect of sacramental worship and the Daily Office throughout. But in the practice of prayer the Office makes a simple, yet crucial, contribution that more exclusively corporate and sacramental worship cannot, by providing the sense of a personal, animate, conscious Presence as the object of prayer. Every Christian knows, theoretically, that when we pray, God listens. But, at the practical level, this idea is easily lost in the multiple considerations involved in liturgical worship, even of the simplest sort.

Ask yourself what you were aware of at your last experience of liturgical prayer? I have often asked this simple question of worshipers, and I often ask it of myself. The usual responses are "lessons," "music," "feelings," or "surroundings," but the common denominator in honest responses is that "I am very much aware of my fellow worshipers. I am not very aware of, or conscious of, the presence of God."

This feeling is understandable. It is also regrettable. Every one of us, at Eucharist, has certain inevitable and important foci. We want to hear the Old Testament read well or the organ played properly. We are concerned with vestments, windows, seats, floors. We are concerned, more substantially, with ethical and theological issues. And most important, we are aware of our fellow human beings, the other members of our parish family. None of these elements is trivial; none is to be dismissed. But the purpose of prayer is a good conversation with God, and when God is not a felt reality, a presence, worship becomes little more than a dramatic production, business meeting, concert, or rally.

Practice of the Office can provide a strong counterbalance. Most regular practitioners, even those fortunate enough to belong to a parish that offers it every day, find themselves frequently in situations in which they must pray the Office alone. As I have suggested throughout, this is the nature of the Office. It is designed to be read either privately or corporately. There are advantages and disadvantages either way. In this the Office contrasts with sacramental worship, which must involve others.

One of the advantages whenever we pray alone is that we can "work on" our sense of the presence of God. We can use our will, intelligence, and imagination to realize God's presence more readily than when concerned about the myriad elements of eucharistic worship. It is much easier, in other words, to realize that we speak to God when voicing the intercessions and that we listen to God when reading the lessons.

A good place to begin cultivating this awareness is in the Lord's Prayer. We can pray the prayer very slowly, weighing the implications of each petition as we go. Most of us sense, for example, that "bread" is verbal shorthand for "material needs." As we ask for daily bread, we can call to mind these needs—shelter, warmth, food, sleep, and so on—and imagine, for an instant, that everything hinges on our asking for them. The New Testament often teaches that our needs are there for the asking, but that we must ask, and that we must mean it when we do so.

These implications are easier to realize, at first, when praying the Lord's Prayer in solitude during the Daily Office than when praying it at Sunday Eucharist surrounded by others. Still, offering the prayer as a serious series of requests is what we should be doing at Sunday worship as well. And here is where the Office helps. We can practice this awareness in the Daily Office, then apply it in eucharistic worship, so that on the Lord's Day we find ourselves more aware of God's presence, of God as the object of the petitions and intercessions.

Practicing such awareness can also work well in a small group praying the Office. Many groups have found this exercise helpful: Imagine a beneficent human presence—the mayor, the bishop, or whoever makes sense—and that we are petitioning him or her in person. How does that feel? What would we expect? How would we speak?

Now transfer these feelings and attitudes to the Lord's Prayer. God is just as present as the mayor in that situation. We have it on good authority, in fact, that when two are gathered in Jesus' name, God is among them. Given that reality, how do we feel? What do we ask for? How do we ask for it? When we say, for example, "your will be done, on earth as in heaven," what are we asking for? What will things be like if our prayer is answered? When we say, "Forgive us our sins, as we forgive those who sin against us," what, again, are we saying? What sins are we speaking of? How will forgiveness feel? Are we holding up our end of this proposed agreement?

Such an exercise can have a galvanizing effect on a group. The "direction" of prayer is not changed, but the focus increases. People tend to forget about peripheral concerns—about what the others in the group think about their requests, for example—and to realize God as the object.

Again, this feeling can transfer to sacramental worship. During the Prayers of the People, for example, if we imagine the presence of God and ask what will happen as a result of that reality, our prayers take on a meaningfulness we may never have experienced. Instead of seeming like vaguely pious sentiments or amorphous wishes, prayers become serious requests.

I have also stressed throughout this book the connections and continuity of the Daily Office with the two primary sacraments, baptism and Eucharist. Although no water is involved, the Office is baptismal in its re-forming aspect. Although no consecrated bread is consumed, the Office is eucharistic in its daily offering of thanks and praise. The two experiences of worship are thus complementary. The sacraments sanctify *kairos* time and celebrate the transcendence of God. The Office sanctifies *chronos* time and celebrates God's immanence.

This fundamental concept of the sanctification of the ordinary brings me to my final point. In the preface I noted that long-term practitioners of the Daily Office may come to sense an affinity between praying the Office and basic human experiences: an exclusive sexual relationship over a long time; practice of an art or a skill to mastery; raising a child or mentoring a young person. All these require a daily, or near-daily, commitment. All involve periods of what seems like monotony as well as occasional periods of disruptive challenge. All can eventuate in joy.

This is ultimately the most important way in which the Office can contribute to spiritual life. It is harmonious with traditional expressions of spirituality. It can substantially improve our habits of prayer, facilitate and encourage meditation, and educate us in the hearing or reading of Scripture. Above all, however, the Office strengthens our relationship with God as a living, everyday reality. Christian spirituality is centered precisely in this relationship.

CHAPTER SEVEN

Getting Started

Lord, open our lips.
       —*The Book of Common Prayer*

At the beginning of this book I suggested that for most people the Office is rather tangential—appropriate for a select few, but not for the faithful in general. The Office is seen as something for the clergy, monastics, or the exceptionally faithful. The idea that the Office is potentially useful for anyone—the idea of actually praying the Office—does not occur to most people. But by now, perhaps, you have come to see the value in praying the Office regularly. How do you get started?

In the past, I have often suggested that persons interested in the Daily Office visit a seminary or monastery where it is prayed daily to get some sense of what it is like. I still make that recommendation, but now add a caveat—because, for the individual and for the small group of friends and parishioners praying in any ordinary parish setting, the Office is, after all, not going to be "like that" very much. Most people will pray the Office on their own, at least at first, and therefore the difficulties they experience with the Office, and the benefits they derive, will be different from those available in a large group. Those who pray alone will encounter the difficulties of isolation, of personal responsibility, and the temptation to skip prayer entirely. They will also experience a familiarity, flexibility, ease, and immediacy likewise absent (at first) in a monastery or seminary.

After years of introducing others to the Office, I have come to believe that the best introduction to the Office is to take up the *Book of Common Prayer* and a Bible. Find a time when you can spend ten minutes with these tools, and a quiet place where there is no doorbell or telephone to distract you. For the next seven days, pray the Office. Do not, at this point, involve anyone else. Your immediate task is to become versed in the Daily Office—to learn its technique.

Choose either Morning or Evening Prayer—not both. If you can do so, choose Morning Prayer. Always pray this Office in the same place—do not go anywhere else, unless forced to. Spend five minutes in silence before the Office when possible, but do not consider silence mandatory, only helpful. Do no other preparation, and add nothing to the Office. Follow the lectionary, and select the canticles as appointed on pages 144–45. Use Suffrages A whether you choose Morning or Evening Prayer. Pray three collects each day: the week's collect, one of the daily collects, and one of the prayers for mission. Add your private intercessions after that, and conclude each time with the prayer of Saint Chrysostom—not the General Thanksgiving. These suggestions apply to anyone, including clergy not currently practicing the Daily Office. The daily discipline of the Office, like many other new disciplines, is best taken up slowly and carefully.

This routine may seem artificially restrictive, but it really is not. You are learning to do the Office, and you are emphasizing the factor of stability. Follow this basic, minimal approach for one week. At that time, begin to explore the complementary principle of variety. Evaluate what changes would you like to make, if any. You may now begin to vary the canticles, collects, and concluding rite. You may add silences within the Office. But do not invite anyone to join you yet.

After four weeks, you may change venues, presuming that this move has not been forced on you already. Try praying the Office somewhere else. Try outside once or twice; try it in the parish church instead of at home or work. Do not, however, change the time for prayer: keep this stable. And continue to do the Office alone. You may be tempted to try to find company, but be patient.

After the second month you should keep varying the Office in the ways you have learned, but otherwise keep everything the same. Add one other change, if possible. Once a week, go somewhere else for either Morning or Evening Prayer, somewhere the tradition is respected and where the custom has been practiced for some time. This can be a parish church, monastery, cathedral, or seminary. Be aware that, almost inevitably, the Office will seem strange in the group context. For one thing, all groups develop, consciously or otherwise, their own "customary"—their own set of practices for carrying out the Office. These customs will be unique to the group, and they will not have occurred to you because you do not need them. Second, you have known only the private experience of genuine Office prayer. Now you are sampling the corporate equivalent, and it is in many ways the opposite. As I mentioned above, its strengths are solitary prayer's weaknesses, and vice versa. Do not let this bother you, but anticipate it.

It may be, however, that you cannot find a convenient place where others pray the Office regularly. If that is the case, you might try to find a member of the clergy willing to pray the Office with you—such a person may be surprised and delighted to oblige. If not—if you live in an area where none of this is possible—keep everything stable, but use a different translation for the Bible readings, and add silences after the readings, if you have not already done so. After three months you will be ready to start a group, if that idea appeals to you. If you try this, you may also incorporate musical elements, if that seems appropriate to whatever group you form. Music is optional, and for some groups might be counterproductive; on the other hand, some groups may find it edifying.

At this point—and only at this point—should you add a second Office to your daily regimen, if that seems appealing. I deliberately urged you to avoid the addition for some time, because many people, in an initial burst of enthusiasm, attempt more observance of the Office than they are ready for and quickly burn out. The twofold Office is very difficult for the individual just beginning to use the Office form. After a few months' experience, however, you are in a good position to determine if the twofold Office suits your needs. You might attempt it slowly, starting with the abbreviated Office in the "Devotions for Individuals and Families," but, by now, you have come to understand what the Office is and what it involves, so you may simply want to begin with a full twofold Office. An excellent combination I have found is to pray one of the Daily Offices privately, the other in a group setting (when available).

In three months' time, you will know whether the Daily Office is suitable for you. You will discover whether it is congruent with your spirituality. And if you follow my suggestions in this chapter, you will have varied the Office enough to have sampled its flexibility.

You will have sampled all the canticles, for example, and learned at least two ways of choosing them. You may have tried different translations of Scripture. You will have experimented with silences, and, ideally, you will also have experienced the Office in an established context. This entire book is meant to lead you in that direction—not simply to provide interesting facts about Anglican practice, but to provide enrichment for your use of that tradition—whatever your affiliation might be. In my experience, knowing the history, the theory and rationale, and the theology implicit in any form of prayer deepens the experience of prayer itself.

I hope that proves true for you, and I hope you find yourself called into the fellowship of the Daily Office. For everything in this book is meant as a catalyst to your experience of this rich yet simple, progressive yet traditional, deeply Anglican yet eminently ecumenical approach to daily worship.

"Who Gets to Do This?"
A Colloquium on the Daily Office

In the Daily Office, the term "Officiant" is used to denote the person, clerical or lay, who leads the Office.

—The Book of Common Prayer

This chapter is composed entirely of questions people have actually asked. These questions reflect matters many are curious about, confused by, or simply interested in, and therefore I thought it might be helpful to share some in their original form. Much of the material has been presented in earlier chapters, but I believe it bears repeating in a different format for three reasons.

First, many people will find that much of what has been said challenges, or even contradicts, what they have been taught concerning the Office. That is why many of the questions seem to take the form, "Are you really saying...?" or "Are you sure that...?" Such honest questions, I believe, deserve what I hope will be reassuring answers. The church has experienced many profound changes recently—a recovery of the original purpose of the Daily Office may be among these changes—so it is not surprising that the subject should provoke bewilderment. My intention is to help with that bewilderment by directing specific answers to specific concerns.

Second, many others have had experience praying the Office and have encountered snags and snares along the way. Such people want practical advice. This is a healthy need, and I also want to honor it. Most of this material is not covered in previous chapters, which do not have such a concrete and practical focus.

Third, different people learn in different ways. In presenting the Office in lectures, informal talks, workshops, and individual spiritual direction, I have noticed that some respond better to the full, conceptual approach presented in the previous chapters, others to a more random question-and-answer interchange. I myself often find the question-and-answer portion the most enjoyable and informative—whether I am the presenter or one of the learners. For these reasons, and for these sorts of inquirers, I think it is worth the risk of repeating myself here and there in the following section. I have heard most of the questions more than once. Some, in fact, I have come to expect to hear any time I lead a discussion of the Daily Office. I have not arranged the questions by topic, but rather have tried to reproduce the random progression these questions tend to take. I do not identify questioners, but it should be clear that I have dealt with questions from fellow clergy as well as from laypersons.

I would welcome additional questions concerning the Office. I may be reached at 311 Huguenot Street, New Rochelle, New York, 10801.

Q. So the Daily Office is really a church service for everyone to do every day?

A. That's right. I realize that idea is hard for most people to believe. I think I can help by focusing on the very phrase you use here: "church service."

The Office is a "church" service—but only in the sense that the church is primarily people, not primarily a place or institution. The Office is a "service," but only in the sense that any formally organized—as opposed to absolutely free-form—approach to prayer is a service.

The word *service* conjures images of something much longer and more formal. This is true for me, too: I think of the phrase "Sunday services." The Office can be a formal service, but it can also be brief and relaxed. And yes, above all, it really is for everyone, and it really is designed to be prayed every day. That's one of the reasons the Office is so flexible: it does work in a chapel, but it also works almost anywhere. It can be prayed in a very large group—by thousands at a cathedral on a Saturday, for example—but it can also be prayed by you or by me in private, alone.

Q. I am not sure I would have time. I am already very busy.

A. The Daily Office was designed with busy people such as yourself in mind! That is one of the reasons it can be so brief. I know what you mean, and I respect your hesitancy to undertake a serious commitment that you may not have time for. But I can tell you that in my own experience, the Office helps on days when I am busy. It keeps me centered when things seem to be spinning out of control.

Q. I know you have covered this elsewhere, but, again: how long does it take?

A. On average, fifteen minutes. When time is pressing, ten.

Q. Is there a "lower limit"?

A. Yes, but I hesitate to mention it. The "Daily Devotions for Individuals and Families," a shorter version of the Office, can easily be prayed, even in a group, in five minutes. The simplified Office, another truncation I use, can be done in seven minutes—which is handy when time is precious. But most people I know find, over time, that they can almost always spare ten or fifteen minutes.

You also come to realize that the Office is not something you have to "make time" for—a duty, strenuous and difficult, "good for you" but not "enjoyable." The Office is a joy—not a chore.

Q. Why are you such a proponent of the Office? Why are you so sold on it?

A. Because I have enjoyed it so much over many years. I have no political ax to grind. I have found a source of joy and want strongly to share it with others. And I like nonhierarchical liturgical situations. I like being led in prayer by others.

Q. Who gets to do the Office?

A. Anyone. You do not have to be ordained to participate. That's one of the nicest things about it. But please let me challenge the way you put it. "Gets to do" sounds like privilege, to me at least. Leading worship—any kind of worship—is about service, not privilege. The privilege, which we all share, is in being allowed to, and being invited to, worship God. Certain persons do us the service, the favor, of leading that worship. By a figure of speech we might say, "Serving others in worship is a privilege." The danger lies in forgetting that the statement is a figure of speech and in thinking of leading worship as a matter of honor and status.

Q. But shouldn't the leader be an ordained person? A priest?

A. No. It can be, but it need not be. Any person can pray the Office. Any person can officiate.

Q. Don't they have to be licensed by the bishop?

A. Only if they are going to lead Morning Prayer as the principal service on the Lord's Day in the absence of a priest or bishop. Not at any other time or for any other reason.

Q. What kind of training is required?

A. None. That's up to the local congregation. If, for example, the Office is offered publicly every morning, the vestry and the rector may want to offer training for those who would like to officiate (and potential officiants may appreciate it). Anyone who wants to pray the Office individually, of course, needs no formal training at all—just try it.

Q. But anyone can do it? Is that really true?

A. Anyone who is baptized—which is not the same as "anyone."

Q. Why must a priest "preside" at the Eucharist, but anyone can preside at the Daily Office? Is it because the Daily Office is less important?

A. Let's look first at what's implicit in your question. First, does the presence of a priest make something more important? That would make sense only if a priest were somehow more important than someone else—which s/he isn't. My prayers aren't more meaningful or efficacious than yours.

Second, should we really use phrases like "less important"? I think that asking about the relative importance of kinds of prayer is like asking about the relative importance of vital organs—they are all vital, so the question makes no sense.

But I appreciate that many people feel the weight of the sacramental services more strongly, so let me offer a counteranalogy—a model that might not naturally occur to you. Think about eating meals. What's more important—the occasional family reunion or feast, or your daily breakfast? Socially and psychologically, there's a lot to be said for the elaborate ritual meal, but nutritionally, there's only one answer. The Eucharist is "more important" in that it is a sacrament, one of the two great sacraments, and has a complexity and depth unlike other worship services. The Office is "more important" the way daily nutrition is important, and daily conversations with loved ones and other human beings. But I think that Eucharist and the Office are less alike than the breakfast and the feast. They are two different types of human activity, not options that can replace each other, as, for example, a rich brunch once per month can substitute for a simple breakfast. They aren't the same, although both contain readings and prayers. The comparison is between apples and oxcarts.

Let's return to another implicit assumption in your question. Saying that "anyone" can do the Office suggests a diminished view of the officiant. The officiant should be a baptized person, and a baptized person, if we take baptism seriously, is anything but "just anybody." Such a person is a member of the body of Christ and of the royal priesthood of believers.

Q. Does all this mean my Presbyterian friend next door cannot join my Morning Prayer group?

A. On the contrary, it means she can. She's a baptized person. So she can even officiate if she wants.

Q. But she was baptized Presbyterian.

A. No, she wasn't. There's no such thing. She was baptized Christian. That is the only baptism.

Q. What about my friends who are baptized Catholic?

A. Same thing. They are not baptized Catholic. They are baptized Christian.

Q. What about my Jewish friends? Can they join in?

A. Well, presumably they aren't baptized. But they can "join in." There's nothing in the *Book of Common Prayer* stopping them. In our parish, we have a Jewish friend who comes to Morning Prayer twice a week and seems to enjoy it. She ignores the trinitarian and christological elements, and I think it's just great.

Q. What if they want to officiate?

A. They are not supposed to. If they really want to, I won't mention it if you won't. I doubt that it ever occurred to anyone that Jewish people might want to officiate at the Daily Office. But in our increasingly ecumenical world, it would not surprise me at all.

Q. What do I need to do the Office?

A. To pray the Office you need a Bible (an edition including the Apocrypha) and a *Book of Common Prayer*, and a minimum of ten minutes.

Q. Don't I need some sort of chapel?

A. Emphatically not. A quiet space is nice, as is a place to sit and a place on which to rest one of the books. But even these are not necessary. As I mention elsewhere, I have prayed the Office on a subway train, standing up. And lying in a hospital bed. So have millions of others.

Q. Isn't the service better in chapels?

A. Chapels are beautiful, helpful, glorious places, and completely unnecessary for the Office. When you are with someone you care about, do you wait for a special setting to talk to them? Maybe to propose marriage, to tell someone you're pregnant, to deliver devastating bad news, or to ask an enormous favor. But not for everyday conversation. And that's exactly what happens over time: the Daily Office becomes a daily conversation with God. A particular setting may be helpful, but is unnecessary. In other words, praying in a chapel has its benefits, but so does praying on a riverbank, or in a subway train.

Regular use of the Office in any place tends to sanctify that place for you—makes it a "chapel" in the best sense. There's a small house in the mountains where I pray Morning Prayer on the porch for a few days every summer, and for me that place is transparent with the splendor of light and the company of heaven. This is similarly true for the space at home where I pray the Office on my days off, for the spot in my office where I read Morning Prayer between services on Sunday, and of course for my prayer desk in the sanctuary, which, when I preside at Eucharist on the Lord's Day, is strongly associated with the week's Offices with my friends.

Q. Don't you need special vestments?

A. Not at all. Vestments can be tremendous visual and psychological catalysts for prayer, but for the Office they are optional. I have officiated at the Office, and have sung as a nonofficiant, wearing cassock and surplice, and tippet, or hood, but never have I "needed" these items of clothing. If wearing vestments helps with focus and separation, by all means wear them. In one parish setting, we vested in cassocks for Evening Prayer every day. We found it helpful. But we did not "need" to do so, and we knew we did not.

Q. Don't you need someone else there? I seem to remember being taught you needed at least two people.

A. Not for the Office. For the Eucharist or for any other sacramental service, you do need at least two people. That is a fundamental difference between the two kinds of prayer. The Office may be prayed by individuals. Then it's just the two of you—yourself and God. But let me add that praying the Office in a group adds a great deal. Share it when you can.

Q. Ten minutes a day does not seem very long. Morning Prayer in parishes I remember took an hour and a half.

A. When you say it doesn't seem very long, is that good or bad? You sound as if you are pointing to a fault. For most of us, accomplishing something worthwhile in only ten minutes is a blessing. At any rate, you are remembering a special version of the Office used on the Lord's Day. That is not what we are talking about. That service is a special use of the Office, but is not the norm.

Q. You say it's not the norm for the Office. The parish I grew up in had hundreds of members. It was a Morning Prayer parish, and that's what these hundreds of people liked. Now the numbers have dwindled, and Morning Prayer, that great Episcopalian tradition, seems to have gone the way of the dodo. Maybe people don't want to have communion that often.

A. Then perhaps they should not. It's not what I'm arguing. I am arguing for Morning Prayer as daily service. That truly is an old Anglican tradition—as old as the Church of England itself. You can pray the Office and still have Morning Prayer in the elaborate way on the Lord's Day, if you like.

Q. But I like the longer ritual that goes with Sunday services. Your idea of the Office seems so mundane.

A. In a way, that's good. I often compare the Office with mundane tasks such as eating breakfast. Think back to this morning. How long did it take to brush your teeth, to wash, to consume breakfast? How many minutes did you spend on these activities? Not many. Yet you probably regard them as indispensable. Such tasks are simple enough for a child to master, and yet they are important. If we fail to perform them often enough, we will suffer sooner or later.

The Daily Office, transcendent and magnificent though it is, resembles, in its day-to-day nature, these everyday tasks. On occasion you will want to savor a more elaborate version of the Office, to take your time. There are many ways of enriching the Office, several of which are presented in this book. I once took part in a festive Evensong that took two and a half hours. But I would not want to do that every day. Have you taken part in leisurely dinners with many courses, speeches, and so on? You may have enjoyed these functions, but you wouldn't want them to occur on a daily basis. Yet you have dinner almost every day.

The key to the Office is not elaboration: it is consistency. This idea is behind the word "daily" on page 35 of the *Book of Common Prayer*. The Office is designed to take place on a daily basis, not occasionally.

Q. What will I get out of it if I add these ten minutes to my already cramped schedule?

A. It's strange, but at first it may seem that you have more, not less, time. But your question is important and deserves a full answer. There is a great deal "in it" for you. I myself, and everyone else I know who practices the Office, do so in part because we get so much out of it.

These benefits, to summarize points made throughout this book, are:

1. Daily strength, confidence, and direction that conversation with God provides.

2. Meditative calm and centering. This has secular as well as spiritual benefits.

3. Daily education in the Judeo-Christian tradition through psalms, lections, and prayers.

4. Daily reaffirmation and reformation of Christian identity, through the repetition of the Baptismal Creed.

5. Daily reaffirmation of ethical and human relationships and identity, through the intercessions and collects and other prayers.

6. Daily celebration of spiritual life and liberty, through the doxologies and other elements of praise.

7. Daily connection with the weekly Eucharist.

Q. What does this last item mean?

A. To connect with the Eucharist means above all that our prayer is one prayer. Our conversation with God is one conversation, although it seems fragmented. One of the most vital aspects of praying the Daily Office is this integrating aspect. The weekly

Eucharist is felt every day. Increasingly, our prayer becomes a single prayer begun on Sunday and continued in the Office.

Q. How does that connection work?

A. Through several means. Most obvious would be the prayer concerns, which are identical, and the Lord's Prayer, which is repeated. The Eucharist and Office also connect through the two versions of the Creed, which complement one another, and through the invitatory, which is a praise psalm. The theme and tone of Morning Prayer is "eucharistic" throughout.

Q. What do you mean by saying the Creeds are complementary?

A. The Eucharist uses the Nicene Creed, which was the original ecumenical creed. The Nicene Creed expresses the collective faith of the church and is most appropriate for the Eucharist, which is always corporate. The Office uses the Apostles' Creed, which was the individual's Baptismal Creed. It predates the Nicene Creed and is more appropriate for the individual affirmation of faith. We are all simultaneously individual believers and parts of the body of Christ. The two Creeds emphasize one aspect or the other. Thus they complement each other, as do the Eucharist and the Office in general.

Q. You are saying, in general, that the Office helps us get our spiritual life together?

A. Very much so. It is an integrating practice. I believe that is very healthy in a fragmented, disintegrating world.

Q. All this sounds good. But aren't you claiming a lot for ten minutes?

A. Yes, but there are many helpful things you can accomplish in ten minutes if you do them every day. Remember that what is important is the consistency, not the amount of time per session. Multiply ten by seven (one week) and ten by thirty (one month) and you will begin to have some idea of the cumulative power.

Also remember that I suggest ten minutes as the minimum for praying the Office, not as an average. Most people take ten minutes when there is not enough time to do more. Most people I know—everyone I know who practices the Daily Office—enjoy it and spend about a half hour at it whenever possible. I do not suggest that amount of time at first, because most people will then rightly protest that they do not have the time. All of us make time for what we find deeply enjoyable, permanently useful, genuinely satisfying. The Office becomes enjoyable for practically every person who practices it faithfully.

The fact remains: pray the Office for ten minutes every day, consistently, over a period, and you will receive surprising benefits.

Q. I tried the Office this morning. I didn't feel these "benefits" you speak of.

A. No, this takes time. I would be very surprised if you did feel the benefits. Some experiences—like surgery, signing a contract, or proposing marriage—have quickly realized, once-and-for-all effects. They alter our lives in revolutionary and immediate ways. A handful of worship experiences fall into this category. But other experiences are cumulative in their effects. They must be repeated over an extended period. Matters of physical health and hygiene are of this nature: you don't brush your teeth once on a certain day and expect to experience dental health. Why should it be different with spiritual health?

A more reasonable approach would be to try the Office every morning for three months. Then tell me whether you have experienced any effects. I would be surprised if you had not.

Q. Three months is a big time commitment.

A. Is it? Only if the daily task is strenuous, and the Office is not. Imagine committing yourself to brushing your teeth every morning for three months—you would think that a small commitment. That's how people who practice the Daily Office experience it—as something they take for granted, as a natural part of their daily life, not as something they must force themselves to do. This relates to the question above about benefits. Regular practitioners are not conscious of "benefits"; they simply do it. They are in the habit of speaking to God in this way once or twice a day—simple as that.

Q. So it's a habit?

A. Yes, it is, but please don't be put off by that word. The word *habit* has developed an almost exclusively bad connotation, but it represents a neutral concept. You and I have many habits we would be loath to break. We might not use that label, but they are habits nonetheless. The Office also is a healthy habit. From a self-centered point of view, it offers nothing but benefits.

Q. When I tried it I found myself busy turning pages and finding my place. Why does it have to be so complicated?

A. It really is not. It just seems that way at first. Again, it takes a little time. I know of no one who failed to "figure out" the Daily Office because of its complexity. Keep at it for a few days, and you'll quickly forget why it seemed so complicated. It's far easier than driving an automobile, and far less dangerous.

Q. What about the great Christians who got along perfectly well without the Daily Office?

A. Actually, most of the "great Christians" through the centuries have practiced some form of daily devotion. These individuals would fall into roughly three categories. If the person—Augustine, Aquinas, Teresa of Avila, Clare, Martin Luther, virtually any Roman Catholic cleric, and nearly all Orthodox teachers—were a monastic or friar, s/he practiced not just the twofold Office of Morning and Evening Prayer, but the seven- or eightfold monastic Office.

If the person were in conscious rebellion against formal Offices, s/he nevertheless would have been likely to practice devotions at least twice a day, including psalms, the Lord's Prayer, and free intercessions.

If the person were a serious Anglican—such as Richard Hooker, George Herbert, Michael Ramsey, Absalom Jones, Evelyn Underhill, C. S. Lewis, T. S. Eliot—s/he almost certainly prayed the Office in some form.

Q. Why isn't that common knowledge?

A. Because these individuals tended to see this practice as something rather small. They do their daily devotions, but doesn't everyone?

Q. I told my rector about your ideas. He says it sounds as if you're trying to turn our parishes into monasteries.

A. I can understand that comment, although turning parishes into monasteries is not my intention! It is true that monasteries use the Daily Office. But as the chapter on history (chap. 1) explains, one of the distinguishing characteristics of the Anglican Communion was the recovery of the Office cycle for persons outside of monasteries.

Q. "It's the same old thing, every day. That's the problem with the Daily Office." That's what my bishop said when I told him about this idea of yours.

A. I wish this were "an idea of mine"! But it isn't. It's an Anglican idea. The most likely individual responsible for it is Thomas Cranmer.

As to the "sameness" issue, a visitor to my seminary from a different Christian tradition once came to Morning Prayer. There he experienced a good taste of what the morning Office can be like, genuinely enjoyed it, felt it to be edifying, and said so. The next day the visitor went through the Office again, then complained, "But that's the same thing you did yesterday!" A friend responded, "That's just the point. We do the same thing every morning. It gives us stability."

That, and a great deal more. The Daily Office imitates, or parallels, the rhythm of daily life. This gives it an almost elemental quality, a "naturalness" that has to be experienced for a while before it is deeply felt, but which nonetheless is real. This is what many practitioners mean when they say that it becomes a part of one's day—not that it becomes a daily habit, but that, like the sunrise, it becomes part of the structure of the day itself.

To use a favorite analogy, although I can hardly claim it as mine, the Daily Office is a work of art. Theologians have often compared God to an artist or poet. After Father and Lover, God as Artist may be the third great metaphor for our relationship to God. One of the ways we experience this, I believe, is through a sense of the creation of each day. Each morning is a work of art, a poem spoken through God's word.

To extend the implications of our metaphor, the regular aspects of the day—the rising sun and progression of hours—parallel a poem's meter. The diverse sequence of events—from catastrophe to elation to boredom—parallels the syntax. Every day the sun rises on good and evil, innocent and guilty. Against that regular background the day is composed as a day of jubilation, infamy, or tedium. The art of the day consists in the tension between the regularity—the clockwork of light and time and rotation—and the nearly infinite variety of possible experience.

Yet each day "the Lord has made." The Daily Office opens and closes each day by reinforcing that rhythm, by making us conscious of it and enhancing our participation in it. The Office puts each day into a theological context that is both unique and the same.

Q. I would like to get the Office started in my parish. What do you suggest?

A. I recommend that you recruit at least five like-minded people to meet for Morning Prayer on weekdays before work—at the same time each day, if possible. Each person commits to officiate on one weekday. Each person also commits to attend at least three days—two days in addition to his or her day to officiate.

One caution: I recommend that you develop a following before publishing a schedule. If you announce the Office publicly you will almost certainly attract visitors expecting a church service comparable to a Sunday morning program. They will be dismayed and confused by the Office. Building a following will also prevent the Office from becoming something the local clergy person goes into the sanctuary and "does," rather than the general practice it is meant to be.

On any given day, then, there will almost always be at least two people present. The lessons are read by whoever is officiating, or by two people, when possible. The officiant should truly take charge on his or her day by determining and announcing which canticles are to be said, by directing the style of the psalm-reading, by inviting free intercessions after the major collects, by observing the silences, and by adding an a capella hymn when that seems fitting. In general, the leader should learn to officiate in an expressive, distinctive, and flexible way.

Q. What about the lectionary? It seems artificial to read set Scriptures each day. Wouldn't it be better to read whatever you feel like reading?

A. First, like any assigned reading, the lectionary has the merits of bringing people together. When you follow the lectionary you realize that many others are reading the same passages. The Bible was written, for the most part, for collective, not individual, reading, so this practice is faithful to this great collection of public books.

As far as individual reading is concerned, you are free to read what you will. Often the lectionary inspires rather than inhibits this response. Those who use the lectionary find themselves drawn into a book and might read it from first to last in a single sitting or piecemeal. But I will guarantee you that you will read more Scripture—a good deal more—if you use the daily lectionary rather than waiting for occasions when you feel like reading a certain book of the Bible. That impulse will not happen often, or at least it does not happen to my friends and to me. Right now, the lectionary has our prayer group reading Judith. It is fascinating to those of us who are reading it, and I'm glad we are. But I would not have "thought of it" on my own at this time.

Q. Isn't it artificial, though, to read the various books in small daily doses?

A. In a sense, yes, it often is. Most of the books of the Bible were meant to be read more or less completely—or at least in much larger bits than we can tolerate. But that's the point. Few of us could afford the time to read what our remote ancestors read, even if we wanted to.

At the same time, there is a great deal to be said for the steady, daily, piecemeal reading of many biblical books. Our prayer group completed Job recently, and the slow, two-week trek through that challenging book was more helpful to me than a three-hour reading from first to last would have been. It kept Job on my mind, more or less continuously, for many days, letting the nuances and problems work through my consciousness.

Modern literary critic Eric Auerbach compared Scripture to a deep, seemingly inexhaustible well in the sense that you may always draw fresh water. Those who read the Bible according to the lectionary will understand exactly what he meant.

Q. You say that the Psalms are read in entirety about once a month, and that they have pride of place in the Office, coming first in the sequence of lessons. Why such an emphasis on psalms?

A. The answer relates partly to the theology of Eucharist. We are made to praise God, and psalms teach us the lost art. But there is more to it than that. The Psalms provide us with an alphabet for the spiritual life; all thoughts and feelings are there. Praying the Psalms daily renews that feeling within us, helping us to express and deal with our spiritual journey. This may sound abstract, or uncertain, to those who have not taken up the practice, but anyone who has said psalms daily will understand. This is why virtually all Christian monastic rules involve daily psalm schedules. They are an indispensable adjunct to intentional discipleship.

Q. The Psalms are in the lectionary. But how do you choose canticles?

A. You could choose canticles at random or make up your own rota. Unlike the Psalms, they are few in number and easy to master. However, the *Book of Common Prayer* (p. 144) provides an excellent plan that distributes canticles appropriately through the week. Following the plan will help the group use the full range of canticles, which are one of the rich resources of the Office. At the same time, even if you use the table of suggested canticles feel free to diverge from it, especially if pastoral or other concerns make another selection more appropriate. Always remember to treat the Office like a piece of baroque music or a jazz score, as suggestive and improvisational, not to be adhered to slavishly.

Q. I see on page 145 a table for Evening Prayer, too. I was taught that the two canticles for Evening Prayer are the Magnificat and *Nunc dimittis.*

A. That's partially true. They used to be appointed for every day at sunset. The current prayer book, as it often does, adds flexibility.

Q. Why is there a list of "suggested" canticles for various days?

A. For one thing, if we choose only our favorites we will never get to know the others very well. Like psalms, hymns, and other poems, the canticles often have to be prayed several times before we grasp them fully.

Second, using a different canticle consistently for various days of the week—and dividing collects in the same way—provides a structure that many find helpful. You gradually come to associate certain canticles with their day—and this provides consistency and order for our chaotic lives. You may argue that you need randomness and surprise; in that case choose at random.

Q. This sounds like one more rigid and monotonous feature of the Daily Office.

A. I don't like rigidity and monotony any more than the next person. But my experience of the Office has not been that it is rigid. Instead, I find the interplay of the canticle for the day, months, and seasons, along with the events in my experience, weaving like music—expressive of all sorts of moods, but with a gentle, strong structure of prayer behind it.

Q. I have a more basic question. What if you don't feel like praying? Aren't these elaborate arrangements then impossible to follow?

A. First, I repeat that the Office is not very elaborate. More important, I have experienced the opposite feeling. The structure of canticle, psalmody, and so on—the shape of the Office—helps you to pray when you don't feel like it. It gives you a language, and an etiquette, of prayer that gets you past mental blocks and emotional muteness.

The early Christians spoke of prayer as an "art." I like that concept. It balances the idea of prayer as a conversation. Think of an art such as playing an instrument—extending the musical analogy I used above. Those who play the piano or the violin practice every day, more or less. They practice whether they feel like it or not and tell me that often they have their best practice when, initially at least, they didn't feel like practicing.

Q. You mean you mechanically read the Office when you don't feel like praying?

A. What happens is that you begin by mentally going through the motions. Eventually, you find yourself praying authentically. The form helps you reach this point. On many occasions, what began mechanically has become real. In fact, the problems that were making it hard to pray came out in prayer. If I had not used the Office, nothing would have happened.

Q. How do you experience the intercessions?

A. One of two things generally happens. Either something on my mind takes over, and I talk it over with God, or I present three thanksgivings and three requests that I have thought about previously. I try to bring these items as my simple "prayer list" every day.

Q. Again, that sounds mechanical.

A. Does it? Don't you make short mental lists of things you don't want to forget to mention to your significant other, your best friend, your coworker?

A. Sure I do, but this is God. It's different.

Q. At one level it is, and at another level it isn't. Let me illustrate. Perhaps you think it best just to pray for the concerns that spring naturally into your mind. That is good to do, and I do it just about every day. But in addition to these concerns, other concerns that I want in my intercessory life work their way more subtly into my consciousness.

My parish is located in an urban area and attracts a steady stream of persons with no place else to turn, who are facing troubles caused by mental illnesses, drug problems, or the law. They see the steeple, come in "looking for the priest," and end up in my office. I try to help them in whatever way I can. I might counsel them or pray; often I refer them to more specialized professionals or to twelve-step groups. Very often I arrange a follow-up appointment with them in my office. Usually they do not show up for this second appointment. Rather than shrugging my shoulders I make the point of including them in my Office prayers for the next two days. That way, I can offer up their name and situation to God.

Q. Can't you experience the benefits of prayer without the structure of the Office?

A. Of course you can. The Office simply acts as a catalyst. The great mystics may proceed far beyond such structures, but most of us are not great mystics. I feel that the advice given to beginners in prayer—"Just let God know what's in your heart, just tell God how you feel"—while it sounds simple, is more appropriate for masters of prayer than for beginners. Beginners in prayer need the structures, routines, memory devices, reminders, etiquette, and language that the Office provides, much as the beginning piano student needs scales, exercises, simple tunes, and basic theory. It is years before she can "just sit down and express herself" at the keyboard. For some musicians, this never happens. And it doesn't have to.

Q. You mentioned "three thanksgivings" in your intercessions. What do you mean?

A. I find it helpful to remember that praise is part of prayer as well as requests. I find I can do this better if I bring at least three specific thanksgivings into prayer each day. We often, even on good days, offer requests and complaints and forget about praise.

We are not good, as I have said, at the art of praise. I certainly am not. But I feel that deliberately bringing three thanksgivings before God each day makes me better at praise. It also makes me happier, which I believe is what God wants and which I believe makes me better at my responsibilities.

Q. Could you say more about this "art of praise"?

A. In the sixteenth century a poem by Edmund Spenser, *The Faerie Queen*, filled hundreds of pages with serious, thought-provoking, and beautiful praise of Queen Elizabeth I. You and I can scarcely imagine even a short poem in praise of a president, a prime minister, or the queen. It is not because we now know about the failings of our leaders, for Elizabethans knew about the failings of Elizabeth. It is because we have lost the art of praise. Most of the time this loss is not crucial. We have also lost the art of dancing the waltz and the minuet, and nobody grieves. But if praise is a lost art, it will be more difficult for us to praise God than it was for earlier generations of Christians.

The same is true for intercessory and petitionary prayer. Naturally there are times when we do ask God for specific help. But more often we are asking God's participation in our lives and God's companionship in our feelings. In our parish we are praying for a man suffering from arthritis. We are not asking God to work a miracle, according to the usual definition of that word, as much as we are asking for God's presence in the medical attention our friend is already getting.

Q. You say the officiant should direct the style of reading of the psalm. What do you mean?

A. I should probably have said *method* of psalm reading. But many refer to this as the *style* of reading. What I mean is that, unless your group decides that a single style is best, you will enjoy a variety of approaches to psalm reading. The *Book of Common Prayer* explains these approaches in detail at the beginning of the Psalter. In a nutshell, they are *unison*; *responsive*, in which the leader (not necessarily the officiant!) alternates verses with the rest of the group; *responsorial*, which incorporates a "responsorial verse" and is not generally applicable to said versions of the Office; and *antiphonal*, the "classic" approach in which verses are alternated between two groups—two sides of a choir, for example, or two halves of a circle.

Q. What if two groups alternate within verses? I've seen that done.

A. I've seen it done, too. But I think the verses' beautiful parallelism is better expressed by reading the verse as a whole, not verse halves. Psalms are written in classic antiphonal, call-and-response form. A silence between verse halves, incidentally, is a helpful practice—simply pause for a beat at the asterisk or caesura between lines.

Q. When should announcements, such as the style for reading a psalm, be made? Should they be made as the service goes along?

It can be done that way, and most groups seem to fall into that practice, but I have had good success with announcing it all—page numbers, canticles, psalms, method of reading the psalm, and other special directions—before the Office begins. In a short time people learn to respond appropriately and to make their way around the *Book of Common Prayer*. It's simpler than it sounds.

I think it better not to interrupt the flow of conversation, and announcements of any kind do exactly that. Thinking again of the analogy to music, you would find it strange at a concert if the conductor kept shouting page numbers, measure numbers, and so on.

A further consideration is that any group that prays the Office often will know a great deal of this information already. They will know, for example, which psalm is appointed for the occasion—no one needs to tell them. They will know the group's approach to psalmody and so on.

Q. What are your suggestions for Evening Prayer?

A. Everything I've said applies. I suggest you consider using only one lesson at Evening Prayer at first. If the desire for a fuller Office eventuates, by all means incorporate the second Old Testament lesson, or a lesson from patristic or other extrabiblical literature. But start slowly.

Q. How about Evensong? Do you have any guidelines to suggest?

A. People think of Evensong as a special event, but it is really Evening Prayer set to music. Nothing should stop even the smallest group from doing either Office with music. Using music is easier than it looks. I did not mention music in the main text of the book (but see appendix D) simply because I am trying to get people interested in daily use of the Office. Many people find music intimidating.

Q. Do we need an organist?

A. No. Generations of monastics sang the Office without the help of organ music.

Q. Are you saying we can't have the organist play?

A. Not at all. If the organist wants to, and your group wants accompaniment. Whatever works for you musically—there are no rules.

Q. What are the rules for the Office?

A. Only what you find in the rubrics. And even these rules can be bent.

Q. In my seminary we always kept five minutes of silence between readings.

A. Yes. That's a good example of a local "customary"—a set of idiosyncratic "rules" that emerges whenever a group worships regularly. The keeping of silence is a rule I highly recommend, and it may be even more important for eucharistic and sacramental worship. Silences are but one example of a rule. Others might be how tasks are distributed within the Office, location of the service, and preferred biblical translations. The only problem with rules is when a group comes to think of its own customary too rigidly or as having application outside its own boundaries. Work out your own customary, without fear and trembling, but don't expect others to find it useful.

Let me suggest something else about the five minutes of silence. Keeping an extended silence is very difficult for some individuals. It is often easier for groups. This is an example of the strength that comes from praying the Office together. To this day, I find it easier to keep one minute's silence in the parish Office than when I pray alone.

Q. Can you tell us the customary in your parish?

A. There are five regular officiants and about twenty people who attend at least once a week. Readers are chosen ad hoc before each session. We follow the suggestions for canticles as printed in the *Book of Common Prayer* (p. 144), which are varied when the officiant wants. The style of psalmody varies. There is one minute of silence after readings. Three collects are the norm; again, this is at the officiant's discretion. Confession is said during Lent and Advent, on Wednesdays and Fridays, and whenever it feels right. We occasionally sing hymns in the Evening Office, and use extrabiblical readings from time to time (see appendix B). All these practices sound much more complicated than they really are. I had to collect my thoughts to recall what we do—it's all automatic to us now.

Q. Do you use a bulletin?

A. No. We think it's a waste of trees! But if you think a bulletin would help, make one. You know your parish, and I don't. You could, if you like, design a bulletin in which all responses and prayers are printed. I do not recommend this, however.

Q. Why not? Doesn't it make the service more "user-friendly"?

A. Again, I think that the difficulty—the "user-unfriendliness"— of the prayer book is exaggerated. Only once have I used a printed version of a rite. That was for a Eucharist where there were no prayer books available.

Q. I have noticed, praying with you, that you don't use the *Book of Common Prayer* much.

A. In time, you learn the "ordinary" part by heart—opening rite, Creed, Lord's Prayer, suffrages, daily collects, closing rite. Gradually you learn all the canticles. Eventually I would like to know the Psalms by heart, but that takes a long time. In time, the collects also become very familiar. I've never tried to memorize any of the material. It just seems to happen. And knowing the material well makes the Office even better. You can pray sentences you know by heart better than sentences you read.

Q. Would you consider using the 1928 prayer book some of the time?

A. No. Only because we do not speak Elizabethan English accurately. And that is dangerous when praying seriously. We should mean what we say—not enjoy how it sounds.

Q. What do you mean?

A. I refer, for example, to the use of *thou*, its derivatives, such as *thee*, and so on. In 1549, these were intimate, familiar pronouns. Now they sound lofty and majestic. In 1611, they were the last words you would have used in addressing King James!

Q. As a priest, I feel I should be in charge.

A. You enjoy leadership, and that's good. But I find that the priesthood entails so much leadership responsibility that it's nice, on occasion, to be led. Good leadership implies the ability to be a good follower. And for priests, opportunities to be led in worship are rarest of all. The Office gives us that opportunity!

I've also heard priests complain that they don't get to read the Old Testament lesson at Eucharist, and now that deacons are used more frequently they don't read the Gospel either. If you share the duties of the Office, you will have the chance to read any part of Scripture. More important, you get to enjoy being led in worship. Psychologically, this practice is one of the ways the Office complements the Eucharist.

Q. Speaking of Bible reading, which translations do you recommend?

A. The *Book of Common Prayer* tells you which translations can be read publicly, and it is a fairly comprehensive list. Privately, you may read any translation, or use the original languages. I've seen people at public worship follow in Hebrew or Greek. It works, as long as the original languages are not consulted slavishly, as long as you don't read in a scholarly way.

Q. Meaning?

A. The best way to read, or hear, Scripture in the Office is in a meditative, imaginative, or practical way. Scholarly questions that come to the trained theological mind should be relegated to some other time.

Q. What do you mean by "meditative, imaginative, or practical" ways of hearing Scripture?

A. By "meditative" I have in mind the Benedictine approach well described by Jean Leclercq in *The Love of Learning and the Desire for God*. In this method, one savors bits of Scripture, repeating them in order to extract their spiritual nutriment. By "imaginative," I refer to the Ignatian way, whereby one pictures the text using the sense of sight, hearing, and so on. By "practical," I have in mind the Salesian tradition of "taking a bit of Scripture with you," carrying it throughout the day, and forming resolve to act upon it. All three have been grouped under the category of "meditation," and there is considerable overlap. I do not intend a rigid description. For some, the best approach is to allow Scripture to work.

In short, I mean that the Office is normally not the time for scholarly research or intellectualizing.

Q. What do you think of embellished or amplified approaches to the Office, such as Howard Galley's *The Prayer Book Office* (San Francisco: Harper, 1980)?

A. I have used them and commend them as long as the eight precepts in the introduction to the present volume are kept in mind. The difficulty with an amplified Office is that it begins to exclude. When one has time, such an enrichment can be a blessing. When it displaces the simplicity of the Office, an amplified approach becomes a curse.

I do not wish to discourage anyone who wants to practice a thirty-minute Office each morning, whether by praying the Office more slowly and punctuating it with long silences, or by embellishing it as Howard Galley suggests. In fact, I consider these methods "ideal" approaches to the Office. But I do not wish to discourage anyone from praying the Office, and I fear that a daily practice lasting a minimum of a half hour would do that. Most important, I insist that ten minutes, or even seven minutes in the most pressing circumstances, praying the Office each day is infinitely better than nothing, and is also better than lengthier approaches practiced sporadically. I suggest that even those with the time to enjoy an enriched Office should occasionally pray the unadorned version.

Conversely, I recommend that anyone, however busy, who practices the ten-minute Office enjoy a corporately conducted Office from time to time at a cathedral, seminary, or parish.

Q. Can you offer other suggestions on supporting the Office in a parish?

A. One simple tool is to publish the weekday lectionary, along with suggestions for canticles and collects, in the Sunday bulletin. I have found that this gesture encourages many to develop the habit. Even though looking up the readings (on pages 936–1001 of the *Book of Common Prayer*) seems easy to anyone who has tried, it seems daunting to anyone who has not. We want as few obstacles in the way as possible. More important, such listings serve as a reminder that the Daily Office is "there" and that others in the parish are praying it.

Another bulletin item I have found useful is a brief statement of the simplified Office, including the readings, Creed, Lord's Prayer, Collect of the Week, and individual intercessions. To anyone who prays the Office regularly this item may look inadequate, but I have seen this simplified Office serve as a conduit for many into regular practice of the full service. As I have implied throughout, most people are very jealous of their time—and this is not altogether bad. Providing a taste of the Office can lead easily to the awareness that it is worth that time.

Occasionally the Office should be mentioned in announcements, lectures, and discussions. Speak about the Office as though it is taken for granted. Allude to it in sermons by mentioning a recent reading, "As we read in the Book of Hebrews at Morning Prayer last Tuesday…" Such allusions will happen automatically, so there is no need to be artificial. The priest or bishop who prays the Office daily sees its relevance almost immediately.

Those who pray the Office within a parish should recognize one another and talk about it. Again, this will happen naturally. Any group that shares a daily practice tends to cohere.

When meetings or special events draw segments of the parish family together at odd times, begin the day or evening with the Office. Those already praying the Office will appreciate the service, and those who are new will be invited into the practice. It is unnecessary to have the rector officiate. At a vestry meeting, for example, one of the wardens could officiate. At organizational meetings, the appropriate officiant would be the president.

During a quiet day or retreat, the minor Offices such as the noonday service, Compline, and so on can be employed usefully. The noonday service provides collects appropriate for mid- and late afternoon, if more Offices are desired. In such cases, several people can share the task of officiating. Lection tasks can be similarly divided among those who may not serve as Sunday lectors. These opportunities can provide a less threatening initiation into either task.

Our parish feeds the hungry at noontime twice a week. We begin with the Office, praying for our parish to be a blessing to many. All who prepare and serve the meals are encouraged to attend the fifteen-minute Office, and most do. The deacon who directs our outreach efforts officiates, and the rest of us, including me, share the job of lector.

Q. We have instituted the Daily Office in our parish. I have noticed that it feels strange now when I read the Office privately.

A. That's because, in one sense, it is strange. It means your sensitivity to the Office has developed in one of its intended directions. The Office, although simple in form and brief in nature, although deliberately nonclerical in application, remains corporate rather than private in character. More precisely, there is and always has been a creative tension within the Office between public and private. Even its ancient Judaic roots contain an amalgam of private devotional practice and synagogue custom. The Office— unlike the Eucharist, which is entirely corporate—stands always on the border between individual and group practice, between private and public worship.

What probably feels awkward are points in the service at which it seems that someone else should be heard and when you address someone who is not there, as in "The Lord be with you" before the intercessions, and where responses are indicated. It may also seem as though someone else should be doing the readings.

There are several good responses to this awkwardness, and one bad response. The bad response is to decide that the Office cannot work unless a congregation is present and to give up. That decision more or less replicates the direction of traditional Anglicanism and defeats part of the purpose of the Office, which is to offer a structure for private devotion.

One good response is to ignore the awkwardness and to read the Office as though others were present. I have known many priests, particularly those who felt that reading the Office daily was part of their priestly identity, who find this method helpful. A second response is to modify the Office by omitting corporate elements, such as "The Lord be with you," when they occur. This practice eliminates the need to imagine others present and the appearance of talking to oneself.

A third response is to use the forms for "Daily Devotions for Individuals and Families" (*BCP* 136ff.). These forms appear simpler than the Office at first. If, however, you follow the rubrics (p. 136) and substitute the appointed lectionary readings and collect and add canticles, the result will be a form like the full Office. In fact, the Daily Devotions quickly become monotonous without such variety.

The fourth and probably best option is to discover your own community. That you are experiencing the solitary Office as strange may be a sign that the time for this move has come. If you pray the Office at home, for example, invite someone else in your household—spouse, parent, significant other, child, sibling, room-mate—to join you, or, if you live alone, a fellow apartment dweller or next-door neighbor. Or arrange for a friend or fellow parishioner to join you at a mutually convenient spot. For that matter, you might consider asking your rector to join you. There is a strong possibility s/he already prays the Office in some form privately and would welcome the company. If you happen to be the rector your-self, you might invite fellow presbyters to join you in addition to fellow parishioners.

This communal gathering does not have to take place daily. You could set up a corporate Office twice a week and continue individ-ual use the other five days. The natural flexibility of the Office makes almost any permutation workable. All groups, however, should emphasize that on the days they do not meet that all read the Office privately. That way, continuity of the lectionary and the intercessory urgency are not compromised.

Q. What do you mean by "continuity of the lectionary" and "intercessory urgency"?

A. The readings are arranged on a daily basis, continuous in nature. While we cannot help but break the continuity sometimes, it would be ridiculous to break the continuity regularly. And, with regard to the second term, our daily prayers are urgent. There should be urgency about our conversation with God. The longer we practice the Office the more obvious such ideas become and the less they need arguing. When we pray the Office with others, their urgency, concerns, and vision complement and broaden our own. Knowing that others close to you are praying the Office even when you must pray it in solitude is strengthening.

Q. I would be a little embarrassed to ask someone else to join me.

A. That's understandable. But how would you feel if an acquaintance, a practicing Muslim, asked you to join him or her for one of their prayer Offices, which occur five times per day? Would you really be offended, or would you be intrigued, flattered, and honored? I can honestly say that, in the past twenty years, only once has someone declined the opportunity to pray the Office— once in twenty years.

Q. What if I don't say the prayers or other materials but read the lessons in the lectionary?

A. I've known several people who do that. It's an excellent daily reading plan for Scripture. But please consider that by choosing the lessons alone, you are saying that Bible reading is the most important aspect of the Office. What this means to most people with whom I've talked is that their intellectual development is paramount. Often these are the persons who need to cultivate other aspects of the life of prayer. By doing only the lessons, you deprive yourself of your half of the conversation. Why not add your concerns, your worries, and your happiness?

Q. I have noticed that the "Daily Devotions" section contains a longer version of the initial words, "Lord, open my lips."

A. The opening words are taken from Psalm 51. The Daily Devotions, truncated in other ways, have included a few more verses. This slight expansion is a good idea from time to time. It helps reinforce the overwhelmingly biblical nature of the daily Office. We can also use all of Psalms 95 and 96 for the invitatory psalm.

Several rubrics throughout the prayer book direct us to expand or shorten readings at our discretion. This direction applies to the Eucharist and other sacramental services as well as to the Daily Office, and seems to be underemployed. Especially while reading the Office, we find that certain "pockets" of Scripture have been omitted in the regular reading plan. These can be recovered. Any time we feel that we want more, we can extend a lesson. Often this extension will mean that the lesson is partially repeated the next day, but there is nothing wrong with that.

Q. I noticed something interesting about the lessons. At the Eucharist on Sunday the deacon who reads the Gospel says, "The Gospel of the Lord." But we don't say those words at Morning Prayer, although the reading sometimes is taken from the Gospel. Why?

A. The Eucharist is a sacrament, and distinguishes among scriptural readings in a sacramental way to emphasize the interrelation of elements. So the final reading is a climactic Gospel lesson, anticipated by the Old Testament lesson and clarified by the New Testament lesson. At the Office we read three (or four) sequential, undifferentiated readings.

Another way of answering your question is to point to the different origins of the two services. Eucharist, although repeated regularly, derives from celebrations of special occasions with specific readings. The Office derives from daily prayer services that offered undifferentiated readings in course.

Q. Speaking of awkwardness, I recently attended a choral Evensong on a Sunday afternoon. Having prayed the Daily Office with a small group for several weeks, that approach seemed strange.

A. That's because Evensong *is* strange in its way. Not "wrong" or invalid, but off-center. Evensong, if practiced only occasionally, is an eccentric version of the Office. It violates the cumulative, daily, sequential principle, and stretches the tension between private and public by emphasizing the public dimension. The strangeness of Evensong is the opposite, in other words, of the strangeness one feels when reading in isolation. Evensong can take on so much of the weight and character of a principal service on the Lord's Day that many worshipers feel tempted to substitute it for the morning service, as in, "I'll go to church this evening instead of this morning." This response should be anticipated and discouraged.

None of this means that it is bad to have Evensong, merely that the service should be understood as an unusual version of the usual—a special version of a daily practice. An occasional elaborate choral Evensong—or, better, a regular service of this kind—may enable us to notice aspects of the Daily Office that normally go unnoticed. Evensong can also serve as a consciousness-raising promotion of the Daily Office.

The only undesirable approach would be to limit exposure to Evensong, as though it were to be practiced less frequently than the Eucharist rather than more frequently. An occasional, elaborate version of the Office on late Sunday afternoon, while lovely, does not provide a good example of the Daily Office in practice. It is a permutation, not a paradigm.

Whenever our parish offers Evensong of this type we embed a message in the bulletin—"Try this again tomorrow, at home." And we include the usual directions on how to practice the Office.

Q. You're saying that the norm is Evening Prayer every day, and Evensong is the aberration?

A. No, Evensong is not an "aberration." It just isn't the norm. The daily practice of Evening Prayer is the standard suggested by the prayer book, envisioned by the Reformation-era founders of Anglicanism, and prayed by many persons. Few parishes, however, offer Evening Prayer as part of their regular schedules. I encourage parishes to try. Given a sufficient number of persons, nothing can stop parishes from doing the service as Evensong. For that matter, nothing can stop any group from conducting choral Morning Prayer, or "Morningsong." But outside of monastic communities, this service is rarer than Evensong.

One fact groups should realize is that adding music increases the length of the service by about one-third. For a short time our parish tried holding a choral Morning Prayer once a week, but abandoned it because it took too long, lovely and easy though it was.

Q. It was easy?

A. All it took was a hymnal. We used simple chant settings and used hymns everybody knew so we could sing them a capella. There was one strong singer in the group—strong in pitch and so forth—who anchored the singing.

My primary point, which is worth restating, is that sporadic use of the Daily Office, morning or evening, violates the service's fundamental principle of stability and sequential progression. This is what makes such choral services strange or abnormal. A group that wants a chanted form of the Office should decide to do it regularly, on the same day or days of the week, for a number of weeks, until it can be done as easily and with as little preparation as the spoken version. You should be able to drop in for Evensong and just do it. It should not require rehearsals. If your parish sings the Eucharist, how often do you rehearse the chants? Never, in all probability.

Q. What preparations normally take place for the Daily Office, excluding Evensong or a special service?

A. All that is required is for the officiant to select canticles and to determine the psalm and for the lector to secure the readings. If hymns are desired, a cantor or the officiant should select them. This process ought to take about five minutes.

Q. I have been attending Morning Prayer at a parish that offers it every day. I find this practice helpful, as it provides a quick prayer service before work. The benefits you have claimed seem to be coming true, and I am happy. I am new to this tradition, however, and I have noticed that the six or seven people who also attend regularly make gestures as they pray. I cannot find these gestures described in the prayer book, and they are not explained elsewhere in your book. What are they, how do you do them, why are they done? Are they required? Are they necessary?

A. Last questions first—no, they are not required and, no, they are not necessary. I have noticed, however, that many people who begin praying the Office end up adopting the gestures. But others do not. Most gestures are deliberately omitted from the *Book of Common Prayer*, even as suggestions, because they have been controversial and probably misused in the past and because the prayer book serves primarily as a guide to the words, not the gestures, of prayer. The prayer book provides for the essential gestures only, such as standing for prayer, and the sign of the cross on the forehead of the newly baptized.

Some people find gestures almost indispensable for prayer. Some, by contrast, have found them counterproductive. My suggestion is that you learn the gestures, try them for a substantial period, and retain them if you find them helpful. Discard them if you don't.

Q. So what are the gestures?

A. What follows is a fairly complete list. Most people who employ gestures use all of these, rather than some.

1. At the opening words, "Lord, open our lips," a cross is traced on the mouth. This benediction dates to monastic practice, when the opening words of the Morning Office literally broke the verbal fast of the preceding night.

2. At the words "Glory to the Father, and to the Son, and to the Holy Spirit," called the *lesser doxology* in liturgical study, one bows

at the waist (not the head alone). This is a more ancient gesture than tracing the cross at the opening, reflecting the supreme worship accorded to God alone and parallel with theological disputes through the ages. It is a very moving gesture especially when done fully, rather than in a perfunctory way. Customarily, this gesture is performed every time the lesser doxology is spoken, which is several times during the Office. Sometimes one bows at the words, "Let us bow down," in Psalm 95, and at other times when the text suggests bowing.

3. At the beginning of canticles from the New Testament, such as the Song of Zechariah and the Magnificat, it is customary to make the full sign of the cross, touching forehead, shoulders, and sternum. This gesture acknowledges the New Testament origin, and dates from medieval practice.

4. At the mention of "life everlasting" in the Creed, the sign of the cross is made. This consigns oneself into God's hands.

5. During prayers people are instructed to "stand or kneel." This rubric indicates a preference for standing. Otherwise "kneel," going in alphabetical order, would come first.

6. It may be customary to conclude the Office with the sign of the cross while saying one of the three suggested versicles. The gesture was probably associated originally with the first versicle, which uses a trinitarian formula, and spread to the others.

7. The head may bow throughout the service at mention of the name "Jesus." This gesture, in contrast to the bow at the lesser doxology, is best done subtly.

Q. I have been praying the morning Office for about three months. At this point it is beginning to seem a little boring. Is this normal, and is there anything I can do about it?

A. First of all, are you really doing the same thing each morning? The psalms and lessons change every day. The collect changes at least once a week. Intercessory prayers can change as often as you like, and you can vary the regularly recurring prayers as well. For example, you can change the seven set collects according to the days of the week and vary the service's opening and closing in all sorts of ways. Except for the weeks after Pentecost, seasonal changes also occur every few weeks. These, too, cause significant changes in the texture of the Daily Office.

All of these variables should provide considerable variety. Are you sure you have been taking advantage of them? I have noticed that people often drift toward a routine that blinds them to these options. Has this happened to you?

If not—if none of these considerations applies and you already are exploiting the variety the *Book of Common Prayer* provides— then it is time to exercise ingenuity. Consider, for example, using the supplementary resources for enriching the Office mentioned in these appendices, either the expanded Office or additional readings. Consider changing venues. If you are praying privately, find a community or invite a friend to join you. Find a parish or place where the Office is already prayed. A new setting will do some things differently, and you may find this refreshing.

Try small changes in your private approach. For example, change the hour at which you pray. Pray the Office an hour earlier, or later. Pray at sunrise, facing east. Pray the Evening Office at sunset. Change your venue for private prayer. If you have been praying at your desk, try praying in the attic or basement or dining room. On the other hand, if you have not settled into a regular place, try to establish a prayer desk or corner. Invent your own small chapel with Bible, *Book of Common Prayer*, seat, table, cross, icons, whatever.

Change your pace. Try reading with exaggerated slowness. Lengthen (or introduce) silences. Introduce a hymn at an appropriate place. Read it silently, as a poem.

Try a different translation of Scripture. This can be a refreshing and for most people an unexpected change. If you know a language other than English, try reading lessons in that language. You will find yourself noticing things you never noticed before.

You might also try consciously retaining a phrase or image from the Office and recalling it through the day—a line from a psalm, for example. Try writing it down and placing it in your pocket, or memorize it. You will be surprised what happens if you keep a line from a psalm in mind. Such simple devices can give focus and purpose in themselves and can transform your experience of the Office.

There are many ways of adding variety to your experience of the Office. It need not be the "same thing every day." Use these suggestions, but better still use your ingenuity and imagination. The only danger is that you might distort the balance in the opposite direction and lose the regularity and continuity that the "sameness" of the Office preserves.

Q. I have used the Office for many years, but now and then there are times when I feel I can't pray.

A. The Office can do wonders in carrying us through ordinary dry periods. But the phenomenon you present is more serious still. At such times you need help. Think of the analogy of the Office as talking to someone you love. In ordinary life aren't there times when you refuse to talk with spouse, significant other, child, parent, or sibling? At such times the relationship needs help from a third party. That's why spiritual advisers and confessors are available.

Q. I'm a diocesan bishop, and I've prayed the Office daily since my ordination to the priesthood. I'm intrigued by your ideas, and I wonder if you would have suggestions about implementing them on a diocesan basis. I'm leery about "legislating" anybody's prayer life, but I would like it if more people and parishes got the idea.

A. Again I have to demur about "my ideas." Almost nothing I say about the Office really is "my idea." But I'm glad, and grateful, that you would like to see the Daily Office more thoroughly diffused throughout your diocese.

In the early church, bishops above all represented unity—theological, administrative, spiritual. And while I agree that legislating spirituality is almost pointless, I have often noticed that the bishop can do a great deal by force of example. Your actions speak loudly. If you let others know about your prayer life—which you may be reluctant to do initially, for good reasons—others will follow suit or be strengthened in their own life of prayer. I have known four bishops who have mentioned their daily practice of the Office. Almost everyone appreciates that bishops are busy and have onerous responsibilities. That one in such a position nevertheless takes the Office seriously and practices it lends it credibility.

One simple idea is to discuss and describe your prayer life, especially your use of the Office, in the diocesan newsletter. Tell people where you pray the Office, when, with whom, and with what embellishments. This offering can serve as an adaptable model for lay and clergy alike—and it *will* serve that purpose, even if you don't express this as a reason for sharing.

Q. I sort of miss the old idea that clergy were bound to read the Office.

A. I sort of miss it, too. It got a lot of people praying the Office, even if unwillingly. But I am glad the stricture is gone because it suggests that the Office is clerical in nature, which it isn't. I miss the rule in that I wish every ordained person, deacon, bishop, or priest would avail him or herself of the uniquely Anglican blessing of daily prayer in this mode. But I think the obligation died for the right reasons. The Daily Office has more to do with baptismal covenant than with ordination.

Q. Would like to see everyone praying the Office?

A. I would like to see every baptized person discover the riches of daily prayer life in some form. Since the Office and its variations provide a tried and true approach, why reinvent the wheel?

Q. Everything you have said makes sense. Yet I can't get away from the thought that repeating words by rote isn't prayer.

A. You're right, it isn't. But that's not what praying the Daily Office is. That's one reason I try to use exactly that phrase, "*praying* the Daily Office"—not *saying* it, *doing* it, *repeating* it, or any other mechanical synonym. Those of us who pray the Office soon become aware of that mechanical danger and take care of it. I have not known anyone—not one person—who regularly prays the Office in rote fashion. Everyone goes through the mechanical stage, like learning scales on an instrument. But nobody stays there forever. Either you get beyond it, usually quickly, or you abandon the practice. To read the Office by rote for very long would be an enormous and unethical waste of time. Anyone who could not get beyond the mechanical stage would rightly give it up. One of the things I hope to do is to help others get beyond the mechanical stage.

Let me offer two further responses to and reflections on your comment. The first goes back to some of the first things I said. When you say "good morning" to a friend, is that "repeating empty phrases" or conversation "by rote"? Is it "vain repetition"? Of course not—yet you say it every day.

Much familiar and friendly conversation is a gesture. It does not convey meaning in the usual sense, but rather acknowledges the presence of the other person. A great deal of the Office accomplishes that purpose—it gives us formal structures for talking to God. We flesh out these structures as we continue the conversation and add the real concerns by means of intercessory prayers and so forth.

But this process takes time. You can't establish a deep conversation the first time you try the Office. It will seem like rote prayer for a short while. But once you learn the language of the Office—and by this I mean not the words, which are simple, but the structures—you will begin to have a daily conversation with God.

This statement raises a second issue. I believe that no matter how sincere we may be, group prayer tempts us to focus more on the presence of other humans than on God. As I said in chapter 6 on the spirituality of the Office, this tendency is most evident in sacramental prayer, which tends to be elaborate, but is also true in the simplest of Office settings—whenever someone is praying with you.

The temptation can even exist when praying alone, when solitary prayer becomes a meditative session or learning experience—especially when one uses the lectionary only and leaves out the prayers. This can happen to anyone, even to those who pray the Office regularly. It is not the same thing as "rote" praying, but is a much more subtle problem.

The first antidote is to be aware of the problem. The second is to try to imagine God's presence. Imagine what it would be like if someone else—the mayor of the city, let's say—were in front of you. You could have whatever you asked for. What would that feel like? What would you say? How would you say it?

The same questions are relevant when addressing God—just more so.

Readings from the Fathers and Other Enrichments

As noted in a discussion of the lectionary, our current *Book of Common Prayer*, and the tradition in which it stands, permits and even encourages the use of nonbiblical readings, thus incorporating an early monastic enrichment as an option for today's church. The appointed daily lections are three in number. Therefore an obvious place for a nonbiblical reading is as the second reading in the Evening Office when four daily readings are desired. This practice is opposed to a second Old Testament reading borrowed from the lectionary year not in use, as suggested by the lectionary itself.

This allows one to incorporate individual spiritual reading into the Office itself, conforming to the Office's principle of *comprehensiveness*. It allows great Christian, Jewish, or other literature outside the Bible to enter our petitionary prayer lives in a vivid way, and allows us to experience the richness of different traditions together—satisfying the principle of *corporateness*. It also introduces a novel element into the daily prayer mix, conforming to the principle of *variety within regularity*. These reasons, beyond the practice's educational value in making us more theologically and historically literate Christians, make nonbiblical reading another simple, time-efficient, yet subtly enriching aspect of the Office.

Several edifying volumes exist. Robert Wright's *Readings for the Daily Office from the Early Church* offers a generous selection of readings. More so than any similar work, it is geared to the current lectionary and *Book of Common Prayer*. It is also ecumenical in approach, incorporating works from Eastern and Western, ancient and medieval, and male and female writers, bishops, priests, and deacons. I commend it to anyone wishing to enrich the experience of the Office.

The difficulty with any anthology is that it must be organized on a day-to-day basis rather than a seasonal basis. A new reading is offered each day. There is nothing wrong with this approach, except that it violates the Office's *sequential principle*, which, as we have seen, is the basis for the Office lectionary. One of the advantages of keeping the Office lectionary is that it encourages reading entire books of the Bible as opposed to excerpts—however edifying—removed from their contexts.

Occasionally, to offset this problem, an entire work can be used for extrabiblical reading, perhaps for a specific season. For example, a classic from Western spirituality such as the *Confessions* of St. Augustine might be divided and read throughout Lent, followed by the *Letters* of St. Ignatius during the Great Fifty Days. Numerous sermon collections for various seasons, written by Christians from ancient, medieval, and modern times, are available. Groups praying the Office might find these collections helpful during the long stretches after Pentecost. There is no rule against using poetry for the extrabiblical reading. A day-to-day selection of poems by George Herbert, for example, might make a meaningful addition to the readings for the twelve days of Christmas.

Almost any Christian reading is appropriate. My only suggestion would be to choose works that can be understood by those listening to them, that are simple enough to yield meaning when heard for the first time. Among poets, Dante, for example, would not meet this criterion. Only a Dante scholar can read him without pauses and footnotes. John Donne, likewise, is probably too convoluted and puzzling. He wrote poetry that was to be read several times. T. S. Eliot, on the other hand, dense though he can be, yields enough immediate meaning (and beauty!) in his *Four Quartets* to make these readings appropriate for the Daily Office.

Any group praying the Office can make its own choice. Favorites can be shared and alternated. For those who would like a yearlong model, the following readings are suggested. The first deciding factor is appropriateness to the season of the year and also congruence with the biblical readings. The readings have been chosen and distributed to conform in length to the scale of the daily Scripture readings. Like the Scripture, there is nothing sacrosanct about these readings. They can be expanded or shortened at any time.

Advent. William Langland, *Piers Plowman.* This fourteenth-century poem, presenting a vision of the Christian life full of deep spirituality, serious theology, and biting social commentary, is splendid reading for Advent. Its emphasis on the "triple Advent" of Jesus—to the world at the Incarnation, at the end of time, and in the heart of the individual believer—makes it especially appropriate. (There is a good Penguin Books translation by J. F. Goodridge [1978]. The original Middle English version, edited by Elizabeth Salter and Derek Pearsall [Northwestern University Press, 1969], can be read with patience by anyone who has learned to read Chaucer.)

Christmas. George Herbert, *Poems.* The tender yet witty theological poetry of this seventeenth-century "metaphysical" poet, who was also a modest country priest and associate of the lay Community of Little Gidding, is a favorite during the season of the Incarnation. (Herbert is readily available in many editions. A useful selection with good notes appears in M. K. Starkman, ed., *Seventeenth-Century Poetry* [Knopf, 1967].)

Epiphany. St. Augustine, *Sermons for Epiphany.* Augustine's influence on Western theology and spirituality is immense. These sermons express his human-oriented incarnational theology. (Available in translation by T. C. Lawler [Newman Press, 1953].)

Lent. Irenaeus, *Against Heresies.* Irenaeus has been recognized as one of the seminal theologians of the earliest church, if not the most important. *Against Heresies* contains his positive theological vision and interesting refutations of many heresies that flourished in the first few centuries of Christianity. Both aspects of this work have a surprisingly modern resonance. (Available in two standard, if slightly old-fashioned, translations: the *Ancient Christian Writers* [no. 55] and *Ante-Nicene Fathers* [vol. 1]. Both series contain a wealth of material useful for anyone interested in spirituality or theology. The former series is still in progress, and later volumes are up-to-date in all respects.)

Holy Week. Selections from the *Showings* or *Revelations* of Julian of Norwich. This fourteenth-century spiritual classic explores the problem of theodicy (justification of the ways of God to humankind) and the problem of human suffering. (Available in Penguin and Image paperback editions.)

Easter. T. S. Eliot, *Little Gidding.* A glorious reading to spread through Easter Week. Eliot's positive vision of the ultimate reality is the twentieth century's counterpart to Dante's *Paradise*. (Eliot's *Collected Poems* are published by Harcourt, Brace.)

Season after Pentecost. For this season, which stretches roughly half the calendar year, I suggest readings in longer Christian narratives. This is the time for reading Dostoevsky's *Brothers Karamazov*, C. S. Lewis's adult fiction, Bunyan's *Pilgrim's Progress*, or any theologically challenging work of fiction.

A Sevenfold Office
Based on the Prayer Book

The current prayer book, as we have seen, offers two additional Offices, the Order of Service for Noonday and Compline, for the first time. It is possible also to offer a sevenfold Office for a group or community that feels a short-term need, such as during a retreat, and when adoption of a monastic breviary seems unwarranted.

Any community is free to embellish the Office by inserting hymnody at the customary places, for example, or by carefully inserting other prayers and devotions. What should be kept in mind is the optional nature of such embellishments. Too often, these have hardened into rule.

The Offices of Morning and Evening Prayer were constructed originally of elements from the monastic and cathedral offices, and the same procedure has been used for Noonday Prayer. To develop a sevenfold Office based on the current prayer book is therefore easy. All we need to do is "unfold" the elements.

Remember that the prayer book merely offers "suggestions" for the lessons and psalmody for Noonday Prayer and for Compline. Any appropriate lesson may be read. Therefore, groups are free to devise a sequential schedule of readings for any or all of these Offices. Since the sequential lectionary for Morning and Evening Prayer is so well established and comprehensive, however, I would suggest that a group devise alternatives to the suggested lessons, appropriate to the season, and alternate them. A good approach, in keeping with some monastic customs, would be to choose a reading for these Offices for each day of the week, and to use them every day, as some Western monastic rules cycled the Psalms. But trial and error will probably prove the best solution.

Another possibility is to incorporate extrabiblical reading into the Minor Offices. See Appendix B for suggestions. What follows is a brief structure for a sevenfold Office:

Matins. If an early-morning (pre-dawn) Office is desired, the Noonday Office should be adapted by (1) use of the *Venite* as an invitatory, and use of the *Jubilate* at the later Morning Prayer (= Lauds); and by (2) using Psalm 119:161–68; 91; or 77 as the psalm; the fourth scripture sentence from Compline (*BCP* 132); and the "Collect for the Renewal of Life" from Morning Prayer (99).

Lauds. Equivalent to Morning Prayer.

Terce (9 A.M.). Adapt Noonday Office, using first scripture sentence and collect.

Sext (noon). Adapt Noonday Office, using second scripture sentence and second or third collect.

None (3 P.M.). Adapt Noonday Office, using third scripture sentence and fourth collect.

Vespers. Equivalent to Evening Prayer or Evensong.

Compline. May be used exactly as the prayer book structures it.

Music in the Daily Office

Many parishes and other communities have customs involving "solemn" or "choral" Evensong, an elaborated version of Evening Prayer. This is a lovely service for Sunday afternoon. Choral Evensong usually involves the use of difficult and unfamiliar music and hours of rehearsal required to master such music. If understood as an offering of time and talent to God, choral Evensong makes for an edifying spiritual experience.

This need not, however, be the only format for sung Evening Prayer. Evensong is offered every day in some places, and takes no rehearsal. An elaborate Evensong can prove a deterrent to new-comers to the Office, for no one is interested in anything so involved on a daily basis. Simple daily Evensong, by contrast, lies within the realm of possibility for many groups. Having a daily sung service preserves the sequential, cumulative, and daily aspects of the rite, while allowing the beauty and expressiveness that musical settings make possible. At present this practice seems almost universally restricted to monasteries, seminaries, and similar traditional communities—but this need not be the case. No "rule" prevents groups from praying the Office through song.

I do mean "praying through song," not simply inserting a hymn or two into a spoken Office. I mean chanting the opening versicles, invitatory, psalm, canticles, creed, Lord's Prayer, suffrages, and collect.

The one desideratum is a group minimally competent in vocal music. By "minimally" I mean only that they have the ability to sing on pitch and carry a tune. Those who have heard the impressive Office singing in monasteries should not be intimidated. The sound they produce comes from years of daily effort, not from spectacular singing ability or arduous musical training. Chant singing is, in fact, simpler than hymn singing. The range in pitch is smaller, the rhythm simpler, the timing more natural. All that is required is training and practice.

The starting point is the hymnal. The current hymnal, designed to complement the current *Book of Common Prayer*, begins with "service music"—chants and other settings of the "ordinary" of the Eucharist and other services, including the Daily Office. S1 through S66, plus S177 through S288, all found at the beginning of the book, provide the music necessary to sing the Office as outlined above, from opening preces through concluding versicle (the second set of *S* numbers consists entirely of settings of canticles). These settings, plus hymns selected from the *H* material throughout the rest of the hymnal, should provide ample musical possibilities. In time, further options can be explored, beginning with the hymnal supplement *Wonder, Love, and Praise*, and the complementary hymnal, *Lift Every Voice*.[1]

In parish settings where the parish musician is interested in and available for the Daily Office, the next step becomes obvious—ask him or her to direct the music for the daily service. In many cases, however, this will not be possible. Many musicians have commitments besides parish work. Therefore, it may be up to the group to determine what direction the music takes. Usually, this will mean allowing the person with the most vocal competence and/or the most musical knowledge to take over.

Directing the music means choosing the music from the options mentioned above and introducing it. The first task should involve choosing options the group seems likely to master; in general, the simpler the better. The parish situation I am addressing will not need much variety, at least at first. Introducing the music involves playing a melody line on a keyboard or singing it line by line.

To most musicians, this process will seem disturbingly casual. That would be a valid concern if the question were one of performance. But it is not. We are discussing a form of prayer in which music is a means to an end. Moreover, we are not interested in the aesthetic aspect, because participants will be singing rather than listening. When a group presents a musical work in the context, say, of the Sunday sacrament, and the majority listens, artistry should be emphasized, for the offering is an offering of talent.

What I am discussing, however, is praying through song, and that should not involve much artistry. Like the Office itself, which appears complicated at first but becomes easy with practice, singing the Office seems daunting but soon becomes as easy as singing a favorite tune. Groups should feel free to try it and should realize that after about a month of practice it will seem the natural thing to do. This statement applies to the individual as well. Nothing is stopping the person who wants to chant the Office in private.

Notes

Preface: One Friday Morning in Early October

1.   Mike, I think, was using his French prayer book. He speaks French and likes to follow along in French. It helps him keep the vocabulary fresh.

Introduction: The Daily Office and Daily Living

1.   The word *formal* is problematic for many people. It connotes something rigid and repressive and opposed to the Spirit. *Informal*, on the other hand, connotes "relaxed," "comfortable." But the opposite of *formal* is actually *formless*—meaning "chaotic," "pointless." The spontaneous, conversational prayer life of many in evangelical traditions is actually quite formal in its use of familiar phrases and constructions. In a larger sense, whenever we express thought and feeling in words, whether spoken or interior, we are using *forms*—because words are forms, and groups of words give shape to thought. The Daily Office is formal in this sense—it gives shape and form to feeling and thought. It is formal in the same way all art is formal. It is not formal in the way white tie and tails are formal.

2.   The word *deacon* in fact was the Greek word for a waiter.

3.   A *rubric* is a visually unobtrusive but theologically or liturgically important sentence—printed in the *Book of Common Prayer* on facing pages—that guides the services. The term alludes to the fact that in earlier editions these were printed in red. They often contain rather major, often unstated, implications about the relative importance of liturgical elements.

4. Basil the Great, "The Long Rules," in *St. Basil: Ascetical Works* (New York: Fathers of the Church, 1950), 311.

Chapter 1: A Brief History of the Daily Office

1.   The norm, in contrast to our prayer-book norm, seems to have been three times a day.

2.   It goes without saying that no Jew called the Hebrew Scriptures the "Old Testament." I do so for convenience.

3. Monasteries where an Eighth Office was prayed in the middle of the night referred to 119:62: "At midnight I will rise to give you thanks."

4. The diaconate had, by this time, been degraded to its familiar status as a preliminary step toward the priesthood.

5. For example, the *Tres Riches Heures* of the Duc de Berry, one of the most famous books ever produced. Introduction by Jean Longon and Raymond Cazelles (London: Thames & Hudson, 1969).

6. Or other "Order," as we should perhaps say, referring to the diaconate. Most who subscribe to the clericalized Office also subscribe to the medieval notion that bishops are merely elevated priests, not in a separate Order—a notion firmly rejected in the current *Book of Common Prayer*, but still embraced by many, wittingly or otherwise.

Chapter 2: The Shape of the Office as Instructed Morning Prayer

1. The extent of page-turning in Anglican practice is, incidentally, greatly exaggerated. The turning of pages seems excessive and confusing only to those who are new to Anglican worship. Understanding what is about to transpire alleviates this sense and one no longer notices page turning.

2. *Cult* originally was a positive word, but has degraded into a synonym for *sect*, meaning a suspicious, eccentric deviation from a standard of belief and practice.

3. Dix, following an Eastern custom, used the word *liturgy* in his title to refer exclusively to the Eucharist. In the Orthodox Church, the Eucharist is frequently referred to as the Divine Liturgy.

4. See also the reflections on the theology of the Office in chapter 5.

5. The word *minor* is used in the same sense as in the expression "Minor Prophets," to mean smaller in size, not inferior in value or lesser in importance—though Morning Prayer retains a certain primacy as the paradigmatic Office, with Evening Prayer as its logical complement.

6.   This raises a curious point in the history of prayer and spirituality. One type of emotional outburst that most people loosely and inaccurately place in the category of "cursing"—expressions said under stress such as "My God!" or "Jesus Christ!"—date in fact to an early period when they were quite consciously and sincerely uttered as prayers. Unfortunately, they "sound" otherwise today, because they have kept the urgency but lost the theology.

7.   Some modern worshipers, especially those raised in an Anglican environment and familiar with the Office in one form or another, have the impression that the confession is actually the "old" way of opening. It often happens that when the church attempts to revert to an ancient practice, those accustomed to a later practice sense innovation rather than restoration.

8.   The worst insult in Shakespeare is, "You rocks, you stones, you worse than senseless things."

9.   If the *Book of Common Prayer* uses the word *Lord* in an Old Testament passage, almost always the name Yahweh, God's proper name, is used in the original. In the Psalter, the *Book of Common Prayer* follows the Revised Standard Version in printing the word *Lord* in capitals whenever it stands, in theological euphemism, for "Yahweh." The Jerusalem Bible is the only major translation that dares to print the sacred name.

10.   Some readers may still feel uneasy with the spiteful nature of such psalms. Such readers should consider that there is always a mitigating factor. In Psalm 140, for example, the curse is not actually made, but confessed. It is quoted as the object of the statement, "I have said to the Lord…" What is prayed for directly is God's protection. Anyone can, in good conscience, ask God to "keep me… from the hands of the violent," but the dreadful, Dante-esque curse is not part of the direct request of this psalm. It is history.

11.   The canticles are identified in roman type by their scriptural name and in italics by the first few words in Latin. The latter custom comes from the Benedictine centuries, which contributed many details to the development of the Office, including the use of canticles.

12.   Various reasons have been offered for this practice, such the need for an alternative to the Jewish station days of Tuesdays and

Thursdays. The actual origins are unclear. We do know that all major religions set aside days of the week with special significance—not one day only. Much of the self-denying quality that Puritanism has injected into Sunday, traditionally our day of greatest festivity and joy, was in the early church more associated with Wednesdays and, of course, with Fridays.

13. The Lord's Prayer was not always located at the climactic moment. The earliest eucharistic liturgies did not use it at all. See, for example, Jasper and Cuming's *Prayers of the Eucharist* (New York: Oxford, 1980).

14. Even more recent Anglican prayer books, such as the Canadian and the Caribbean, which in many ways have improved upon the American edition, are also traditional in the sense defined here.

15. A handy example is the Eucharistic Prayer. The 1979 *Book of Common Prayer* provides not one, but four, options, two of which are more ancient in content and all of which are more ancient in form than the late-medieval model previously offered.

16. The thanksgiving may have been part of a trial eucharistic prayer, a private prayer for the monarch, or an original composition by Reynolds himself. See the background provided in Marion Hatchett's *Commentary* (New York: Seabury, 1981).

Chapter 3: Evening Prayer

1. One of the earliest poems in the English language, the "Dream of the Rood," is an extended meditation on this paradox.

2. Again, a paradox embraced avidly by poets, notably George Herbert and Richard Crashaw in the seventeenth century.

3. As Augustine first said, and as we repeat in one of the collects at Morning Prayer.

4. A metrical setting, put simply, restates the words of a text so that it fits metrical music—the style of most hymns. The words are adapted to a fixed piece of music. Chant, by contrast, offers music flexible enough to fit a fixed text.

Chapter 5: A Theology of the Daily Office

1. The initial prayer offers another example of the need for contemporary language. The Elizabethan phrase "our mouth shall

show forth thy praise" had meaning in the sixteenth century. It no longer means anything, since we no longer use the expression "show forth." The phrase is in fact confusing, since it seems to mix the visual ("showing") with the vocal (what we do with the mouth in praise). On the other hand, everyone understands what it means to "proclaim." Whenever words are used in prayer because they "sound" more lovely, spiritual, or poetic, but their meaning cannot be specified, we should be on guard. That way lies the way of the Pharisee.

2.   Our usual translation as "thanksgiving" alone is shorthand. The word has a larger meaning than that.

Chapter 6: The Spirituality of the Daily Office

1.   The thoroughgoing materialist from Democritus to Karl Marx will dismiss all spirituality in this sense as delusion or fiction. The thoroughgoing spiritualist, whether Apollinaris or William Blake, will deny that there is anything else.

2.   In the early fourth century, Constantine reversed the fortunes and history of the Christian church by making it (1) legal and (2) official. What had appealed to heroic spirits could now appeal only to the politically correct, the pragmatic, and the opportunist, so the blessing was decidedly mixed.

Appendix D: Music in the Daily Office

1.   *Wonder, Love, and Praise* (New York: Church Publishing Incorporated, 1997); *Lift Every Voice* (New York: Church Hymnal Corporation, 1993).

Selected Bibliography

This short selection of further reading is intended primarily for those who may wish to explore some aspect of the Daily Office further. Anyone interested in scholarly inquiry should be able to find suggestions to get started. *The Study of Liturgy* and *The Study of Spirituality* would be excellent starting points.

As we have seen throughout, the Daily Office is paradoxically both public and private. The Office does not represent a compromise between the two, but is fully useful in either mode. A solitary person can pray the Office as effectively as a hundred people supported by a full choir. Thus the subject pertains equally to spirituality and to liturgics. I have chosen, therefore, key works in both fields. Study in either area will be helpful for gaining a balanced and full understanding of the Office, whether one wishes to pray alone or in a group.

The Office's scriptural emphasis suggests inclusion of a few works of biblical scholarship. Those who pray the Office seem almost inevitably to start asking the questions of biblical scholarship, which are quite commonsense and natural: When was this written? Who wrote this? What does this mean? A few biblical resources, which are included in the bibliographical list below, can help answer such questions.

To begin, however, with basic works in liturgics, *Sanctifying Time, Life, and Space** (New York: Seabury, 1976) by Marion Hatchett (asterisks mark works that I consider essential) is an excellent introduction to serious liturgical study. Insofar as the Office is a liturgical action, Hatchett's precepts are extremely relevant. Hatchett is also the author of the *Commentary on the American Prayer Book* (New York: Seabury, 1981), a comprehensive and ultimately fascinating reference, providing background and sources for virtually everything in the *Book of Common Prayer.* Anyone interested in the history of the Office would do well to start here. Hatchett's developmental charts are especially helpful.

The Study of Liturgy (New York: Oxford University Press, 1992), the first collaborative effort by Cheslyn Jones, Geoffrey Wainwright, and Edward Yarnold, is a superb anthology of introductory-level yet challenging essays covering the entire field of liturgical study. The work is particularly strong in history. Aidan Kavanagh's *Elements of Rite* (New York: Pueblo, 1982) presents a quirky, provocative, but also deeply felt set of suggestions for practitioners of public worship. Consciously designed on the lines of William Strunk and E. B. White's little classic, *The Elements of Style*, it never hesitates to prescribe, condemn, and complain. The work constitutes a very human and humorous approach more applicable to Sunday worship than to the Office, but applicable to the Office as well.

The following is an annotated list of other helpful works in liturgics and spirituality:

Baumstark, Anton. *Comparative Liturgy* (London: A. R. Mowbray, 1958). Difficult, essential text for those interested in worship theory. Much of what others say about liturgy, myself included, is based on Baumstark. He provides ways to understand liturgy in a larger anthropological and psychological context.

Bouyer, Louis. *Liturgical Piety* (Notre Dame, Indiana: Notre Dame University Press, 1955). Although written from an earlier Roman Catholic perspective, this remains an excellent resource. The chapter on the breviary parallels the Anglican understanding of the Office in many respects. The same author's *Introduction to Spirituality* and *Meaning of Holy Scripture* are recommended with the same caveats.

Cullmann, Oscar. *Early Christian Worship* (London: SCM Press, 1953). One key to understanding the contemporary Office is to appreciate the degree to which it returns to ancient Christian forms and practice. Cullmann provides that context.

Cuming, C. G. *A History of Anglican Liturgy* (London: MacMillan, 1982). Especially valuable for understanding the unique Anglican rationale for the Office and other rites.

Dugmore, S. W. *The Influence of the Synagogue upon the Divine Office* (London: Oxford University Press, 1944). Dugmore explores in detail one aspect of the multifaceted Hebraic influence traced in my historical outline.

Eliade, Mircea. *Cosmos and History* (New York: Harper, 1959) and *Sacred and Profane* (New York: Harcourt, Brace, 1959). These essential anthropological studies complement the work of Otto.

Jones, Cheslyn, Geoffrey Wainright, and Edward Yarnold. *The Study of Spirituality* (London: SPCK, 1986). A companion volume to their study of liturgy, this work is equally applicable to the Office, which is, as I have maintained, spiritually amphibious. This work is more logically organized than the other work, tracing the sweep of Christian spirituality from the biblical era to the present ecumenical age.

Legg, J. W. *Cranmer's Liturgical Projects* (London: Harrison, 1915). Examines the complex liturgical experiments that culminated in the first editions of the *Book of Common Prayer*.

McArthur, A. *The Evolution of the Christian Year* (London: SCM Press, 1953). Important for understanding the seasonal aspects of the Daily Office.

Merton, Thomas. *The Sign of Jonas* (New York: Harcourt, Brace, Jovanovich, 1979). This work and Henri Nouwen's *Genesee Diary* (New York: Phoenix, 1985) are surprisingly similar books by strikingly different authors. While practically anything by these popular writers can be recommended, these two journal-like works have a special relevance for the person interested in the Office. Each book contains the day-by-day psychological record of a first encounter with the sevenfold monastic Office. We see Merton's eccentric brilliance and Nouwen's gentle vagueness, each tempered by the humanity of this daily form of discipline and prayer.

Nouwen, Henri. *The Genesee Diary*. See the entry for Merton's *Sign of Jonas*.

Otto, Rudolph. *The Idea of the Holy* (New York: Oxford, 1969). A seminal work on the philosophy and psychology of religious experience that defines the connection between theology and worship in the most basic sense.

Salmon, P. *The Breviary through the Centuries* (Collegeville, Minnesota: Liturgical Press, 1962). The Roman breviary is a spiritual cousin to the Anglican Office. They share the same basic lineage, but are intended for different purposes. Much of the material here is therefore also relevant to the Office.

Schmeeman, Alexander. *Introduction to Liturgical Theology* (Crestwood, New York: St. Vladimir's Seminary Press, 1956). Presents the Orthodox viewpoint. Interesting for its contrast with the Anglican stress on the Office.

Smith, Martin. *The Word Is Very Near You** (Cambridge, Massachusetts:
    Cowley Press, 1989). An imaginative reworking of traditional
    ways of approaching Scripture, integrated with contemporary
    biblical awareness. A contemporary classic and entirely com-
    patible with the Daily Office.
Squire, Aelred. *Asking the Fathers* (Wilton, Connecticut: Morehouse-
    Barlow, 1976). An impressionistic essay on the relevance of the
    fathers for late-twentieth-century readers, this work from the
    early 1970s is already somewhat dated, but remains a healthy
    and creative introduction to the classic era of Christian spiri-
    tuality.
Tugwell, Simon. *Ways of Imperfection** (Springfield, Illinois: Templegate,
    1995). A collection of essays by a monastic and scholar that cov-
    ers the same ground as *The Study of Spirituality*, but in a more
    personal way. A solid and practical introduction to Christian
    spirituality. It could be considered the counterpart to
    Hatchett's *Sanctifying Time, Life, and Space*.

I have stressed the biblical orientation of the Office throughout.
Among many other strengths, the Office invites us into a daily
encounter with Scripture, regardless of our situation and mood.
Those with little background in scriptural study will probably find
that this aspect of the Office makes them hunger for more biblical
knowledge. They might start by exploring the following:

Anderson, Bernhard. *Understanding the Old Testament* (Englewood
    Cliffs, New Jersey: Prentice-Hall, 1966). Both this book and
    Norman Perrin's *The New Testament: An Introduction* (New York:
    Harcourt, Brace, Jovanovich, 1982) provide a starting point for
    digging more deeply into the Bible. Perrin's book is fairly up-
    to-date. Anderson is dated, but so good that it has not been
    superseded. Any solid academic introduction will, of course,
    serve nearly as well.
Bennett, Robert A. *The Bible for Today's Church* (New York: Seabury,
    1979). This teaching-series volume on Scripture is excellent
    and may be more easily accessible than Wright and Fuller's
    Book of the Acts of God.

Guthrie, Harvey. *Israel's Sacred Songs* (New York, Seabury, 1966). Since the Psalms, in the Office, are the most frequently read book of the Bible, many will find a single-volume commentary helpful. This book, along with J. W. Rogerson and J. W. McKay's *The Psalms* (New York: Cambridge University Press, 1977), is excellent. Rogerson and McKay analyze the Psalms one by one; Guthrie provides more historical and sociological context.

Interpreter's One-Volume Commentary (Nashville: Abingdon, 1971); *The New Jerome Bible Handbook* (Collegeville, Minnesota: Liturgical Press, 1993); and *Peake's Bible Commentary** (London: Nelson, 1962). Many who pray the Office, myself included, find it helpful to keep a one-volume biblical commentary handy, as the lectionary provokes questions on serious theological issues as well as on small but interesting details about money, customs, weights, measures, and so forth. These three works are standard and inexpensive.

Lewis, C. S. *Reflections on the Psalms* (London: Collins, 1969). Written from the nonexpert, praying person's viewpoint, this book deals with many of the problems modern worshipers encounter in the Psalms. An interesting complement to Harvey Guthrie's *Israel's Sacred Songs.*

Perrin, Norman. *Introduction to the New Testament.* See the entry for Anderson's *Introduction to the Old Testament.*

Pieper, Josef. *In Tune with the World: A Theory of Festivity* (Chicago: Franciscan Herald Press, 1973). A remarkable essay by a modern Thomist scholar. Combines theology, philosophy, psychology, and sociology to work out a theory of life based on worship.

Rogerson, J. W. and J. W. McKay. *The Psalms.** See the entry for Guthrie's *Israel's Sacred Songs.*

Wright, E., and R. Fuller. *The Book of the Acts of God** (Garden City, New York: Anchor Books, 1960). A modern classic introducing the Bible in light of modern biblical scholarship and theory, while never losing sight of spiritual and theological reality.

Understanding Faith: An Exploration of Christian Theology

C. W. McPherson

Understanding Faith is a book for all
Episcopalians. Using basic and clear
language, and working from the Nicene
Creed and the Episcopal Catechism,
the Reverend C. W. McPherson
introduces the core concepts of Christian
theology. Unlike other books of theology,
this one incorporates twentieth-century
science, philosophy, literature, and
history and draws particularly on Ludwig
Wittgenstein's understanding of linguistic
analysis.

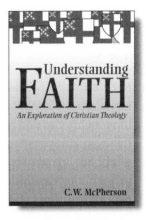

Available from bookstores everywhere or on the Internet at
www.morehousepublishing.com

MOREHOUSE PUBLISHING